Intellectual Property Rights: Protection of Plant Materials

Intellectual Property Rights: Protection of Plant Materials

Editors
P. Stephen Baenziger
Roger A. Kleese
Robert F Barnes

Sponsors
Crop Science Society of America
American Society for Horticultural Science
American Society of Agronomy
Soil Science Society of America
U.S. Department of Agriculture-Science and Education

Managing Editor
N. H. Rhodehamel

CSSA Special Publication Number 21

Crop Science Society of America
American Society of Agronomy
Soil Science Society of America

Cover Design: Patricia Scullion

Crop Science Society of America, Inc.
American Society of Agronomy, Inc.
Soil Science Society of America, Inc.
677 South Segoe Road, Madison, WI 53711, USA

Library of Congress Cataloging-in-Publication Data

Intellectual property rights : protection of plant materials / editors, P. Stephen Baenziger, Roger A. Kleese, Robert F Barnes; sponsors, Crop Science Society of America . . . [et al.].
p. cm. — (CSSA special publication; no. 21)
Proceedings of a workshop held Jan. 26–28, 1993.
Includes bibliographical references.
ISBN 0-89118-537-2
1. Plant varieties—United States—Patents—Congresses.
I. Baenziger, P. Stephen. II. Kleese, Roger A. III. Barnes, Robert F, 1993- . IV. Crop Science Society of America. V. Series.
KF3133.P53I58 1993
346.7304'86—dc20
[347.306486] 93-5949
CIP

CONTENTS

OVERVIEW AND PURPOSE OF WORKSHOP

The right of inventors to secure legal property protection for creative efforts and discoveries is provided by the U.S. Constitution. Within the last decade the options for exercising this right with respect to plant-derived intellectual property have expanded to include utility patents. This has created an array of issues and questions that must be addressed by scientists, administrators, and policy makers. This workshop was organized define these issues more precisely and to encourage discussion and dialogue among individuals and representatives of organizations with different goals and perspectives.

A primary goal of the workshop was to aid in the development of policies and procedures associated with plant-derived intellectual property that are not only publicly responsible, but that provide the incentives needed to assure commercialization of new inventions. A further goal was to frame intellectual property issues in one or more "educational modules" that could be used in informational seminars with various public and private sector groups.

Public and private institutions have invested large amounts of time and money in research to produce more useful and productive plants with unique, differentiated traits. Their research and technology dissemination systems have successfully fostered creativity and discovery and produced genetic products that have helped make U.S. agriculture among the most productive in the world. Procedures, policies, and protocols for protection of plant intellectual property, in both public and private institutions, must encourage this discovery and product development process.

The demands for environmental stewardship, sustainability, food safety and quality, and economic competitiveness pose new challenges. The research system must continue to foster the creativity and discovery needed to generate the superior plant products and services needed to meet these challenges.

Representatives of different institutions and culture bring different perspectives on property protection issues. Through discussion and sharing of ideas, we hope we have come closer to assuring that practices and procedures followed with respect to intellectual property protection will (i) encourage creativity and new discovery, and (ii) promote rapid development of superior new products and services—for people of all nations. If we contributed to this goal, then this conference was a success.

This conference built on the ideas and topics from the intellectual property rights conference at Anaheim, CA, which the tri-Societies sponsored in 1989. While many of the issues were the same, practices have evolved, the state of science has advanced, international relationships have changed, and new issues have emerged. Case by case, institutions have addressed many of these issues in one way or another—some more satisfactorily that others. We hope this conference helped identify what is working and what is not working with regard to plant property protection and what can be done to make the entire system more effective. We hoped to identify particularly difficult issues that simply have not been addressed in practice, make recommendations with regard to institutional policy changes or changes in laws, and identify issues that have emerged since 1989. Resolution of these issues will need input from the university, government, private industry, non-governmental, international, and legislative perspectives.

Real-life examples from key presenters provided the basis for discussions on licensing, exemptions, exchanges, ethical and social issues, and research agenda-setting. Discussion sessions broadened perspectives about intellectual property protection and fostered greater cooperation among institutions and among the public and private sectors. Our goal was simply to make our research and technology system work better.

The steering committee for this conference believed that the target audience for the product of the workshop should be research administrators and policy makers in companies, universities, and government, who make intellectual property decisions and set policies. There were many such people among the conferees. There were also many conferees who are actively involved in breeding and genetics research and who can attest to the impact of property protection policies on the day-to-day activities of researchers. We believe that this workshop was of benefit to all, and that it and this proceedings will help foster more consistent institutional policies on key issues.

PREFACE

This special publication presents a continued treatise on the policies and practices related to proprietary aspects of plant materials. It summarizes the results of a workshop held in Washington, DC, 26–28 January 1993. Over 100 individuals participated in six work group sessions.

Chapters 1 through 10 consist of Plenary Papers which present comprehensive updates and evaluations of intellectual property rights for the protection of plant materials. The remaining chapters, 11 through 17, provide brief vignettes focussed on the five major issues (licensing, exemptions, exchanges, ethical and social issues of protection, and research agenda) that were the topics of simultaneous break out sessions. A workshop synthesis group reviewed the findings of each issue-oriented work group and identified high priority issues and recommended actions for future implementation.

An Executive Summary provides a concise statement of recommendations and a general summary of the workshop. The work group reports summarize the recommendations resulting from discussions centered on addressing the following questions:

1. What are the current issues facing owners, inventors, and administrators with respect to plant derived intellectual property?
2. What practices are currently being followed in the private and public sector?
3. What, if any, changes in practices, institutional policies, or laws might be considered or recommended? Who or what agencies should lead in recommending changes?
4. What educational programs are necessary to better inform important players regarding plant-derived intellectual property issues? Who should teach and who should listen?

The workshop was jointly organized by the Crop Science Society of America and the American Society for Horticultural Science with Victor L. Lechtenberg and Richard L. Lower serving as co-chairs from the respective societies.

Financial support was provided by the U.S. Department of Agriculture, Science and Education; ASA; CSSA; SSSA; and the organizations and individuals participating in the workshop.

The editors compliment the authors of chapters and work group reports for a timely and thorough presentation of the proceedings of the workshop.

Special thanks are extended to Charles E. Hess and Duane Acker, both former Assistant Secretaries for Science and Education, USDA and R. Dean

Plowman and William H. Tallent, USDA-ARS for their encouragement and support of the project.

P. STEPHEN BAENZIGER
University of Nebraska, Lincoln, Nebraska

ROGER A. KLEESE
Pioneer Hi-Bred International, Des Moines, Iowa

ROBERT F BARNES
ASA, CSSA, SSSA, Madison, Wisconsin

CONTRIBUTORS

Alan A. Atchley	Plant Variety Examiner, Plant Variety Protection Office, 10301 Baltimore Boulevard, Beltsville, MD 20705
John H. Barton	George E. Osborne Professor of Law, Stanford Law School, Stanford, CA 94305
Lawrence Busch	Professor of Sociology, Department of Sociology, Michigan State University, East Lansing, MI 48824
Donald N. Duvick	Professor of Plant Breeding, Iowa State University, 6837 N.W. Beaver Drive, P.O. Box 446, Johnston, IA 50131-0446
Barry Greengrass	34 chemin des Colombettes, P.O. Box 18, CH-1211 Geneva 20, Switzerland
Charles E. Hess	Department of Environmental Horticulture, College of Agriculture and Environmental Science, University of California, Davis, CA 95616
Dennis R. Hoerner	Associate Patent Counsel, Monsanto Company, 700 Chesterfield Village Parkway-North, St. Louis, MO 63198
David J. Houser	Patent Counsel, Wisconsin Alumni Research Foundation, P.O. Box 7365, Madison, WI 53705-7365
Bruce Hunter	Head, Maize Breeding and Development, CIBA Seeds, P.O. Box 18300, Greensboro, NC 27419-8300
Richard L. Lower	Executive Director, Agricultural Experiment Station, College of Agricultural and Life Sciences, University of Wisconsin, 1450 Linden Drive, Madison, WI 53706
Terry L. Nipp	AESOP Enterprises, Ltd., 123 4th Street SE, Washington, DC 20003-1013
Eldon Ortman	Associate Director, Agricultural Research Programs, Purdue University, 1140 Ag Administration Building, West Lafayette, IN 47907
R. D. Plowman	Administrator, USDA-ARS, Room 302-A, Washington, DC 20250
Nicholas J. Seay	Quarles and Brady, 1 South Pinckney Street, Suite 600, Madison, WI 53703
Henry L. Shands	Associate Deputy Administrator, Genetic Resources, USDA-ARS, NPS, Building 005, Room 215, BARC-West, 10300 Baltimore Avenue, Beltsville, MD 20705-2350

Keith A. Walker Director, Planning and Licensing, Mycogen Corporation, 4980 Carroll Canyon Road, San Diego, CA 92121

Elizabeth C. Weimar U.S. Department of Commerce, PTO, Art Unit 184, Group 180, Washington, DC 20231

Executive Summary

EXECUTIVE SUMMARY

Intellectual Property Rights: Protection of Plant Materials

A workshop entitled "Intellectual Property Rights: Protection of Plant Materials" was held in Washington, DC, 26–28 Jan. 1993. The participants included 116 individuals from a broad range of disciplinary, professional, and administrative interests. Plenary speakers addressed such topics as goals of inventors, owners, and users; implications of non-U.S. protection, procedures, and practices for U.S. innovators; the status of intellectual property rights (IPR) protection; science-based identification of plant genetic materials; and national legislative issues.

Five work groups (see Appendix 4), each composed of a cross section of conferees, addressed critical issues and problems in the following areas: (i) licensing; (ii) research and farmer exemptions; (iii) germplasm and information exchange; (iv) ethical and social concerns; and (v) the impacts of property protection on research agendas. Each work group was asked to address current practices in both the public and private sectors and to develop recommendations for policies and educational programs that would improve the property protection system and mitigate any negative impacts on research and information exchange among scientists. The deliberations of each group were then summarized and the five highest priority issues from all groups were identified. Recommendations to address each of these priority issues were then developed, along with a description of expected outcomes if the recommendations were implemented.

LICENSING WORK GROUP

Licensing was recognized by both private and public sector attendees as the primary vehicle by which intellectual property rights are transferred from inventors to users. The private sector is generally comfortable with licensing; however, all recognize that there is uncertainty in evaluating the commercial potential of individual plant "inventions." One commonly used form of license is a material transfer agreement (MTA), which usually conveys the right to use plant materials for research purposes only. These agreements are encouraged.

Conferees encouraged consistent licensing practices at public institutions. Companies, however, often do not know what office or person to deal with in universities and often are not informed when potentially valuable material is available for licensure. Public institutions were encouraged to protect their intellectual property positions, and to offer a basis for licensing materials that might have commercial value. It was also recognized that exclusive license agreements, especially if a public institution is the licensor, can create tensions about germplasm access among plant breeders.

The manner in which plant breeders are treated, as inventors, was also perceived as a serious issue. A majority of participants believed it was important to encourage a uniform policy within and among public organizations. Team efforts could be discouraged if breeders and their coworkers are not treated uniformly. In many cases it is extremely difficult to determine "who is the inventor."

Concern was also expressed about the impact of exclusive licenses on the credibility that public organizations have with the general public. It is especially important for public institutions to assure equal access to protected materials and to provide broad-based notification of all technology made available for potential licensing. The goal of licensing by public institutions should be to maximize public benefit; accruing revenue should be a lesser priority.

The licensing work group encouraged significant efforts in education and communication on intellectual property issues, especially licensing within public institutions. All staff should be well informed regarding options for protection, material transfer agreements, and institutional policies.

Lastly, licenses must be enforced. Agreements need a due-diligence clause or march-in clause and prohibitions against transferring licensed materials to third parties.

EXEMPTIONS WORK GROUP

Two types of exemptions are important to plant intellectual property—research and farmer exemptions. Research exemptions allow the use of protected intellectual property for true research purposes, without infringement. Farmer exemptions allow farmers to keep seed they produce from protected materials and use it for seeding purposes in their own enterprises. The Plant Variety Protection Act (PVPA) explicitly contains both research and farmer exemptions. The current farmer exemption in the PVPA allows a farmer to sell significant quantities of "surplus seed" to neighbors, a provision that has been the subject of considerable debate and litigation. It is generally accepted that a de facto farmer exemption exists—saving seed to use on one's own farm—due simply to the fact that enforcement would be impractical.

Utility patent law makes no provision for exemptions, and there has been no attempt to establish these exemptions within the law. Judicial decisions appear, however, to provide an exemption from infringement penalties for noncommercial research. Ambiguities arise in determining what constitutes "noncommercial" research. The same rules need to apply to public sector research as to private sector research, since universities often engage in research that can have commercial potential.

Conferees generally recognized that the current PVPA farmer exemption does not provide adequate protection for intellectual property. As a result, many inventors are seeking patent protection in lieu of plant variety protection. In addition, the current PVPA does not conform to the 1991 Convention of International Union for the Protection of New Varieties of Plants (UPOV). The farmer exemption provision of the 1970 PVPA requires revision so that farmers may continue to keep seed of protected varieties for their own use, and may be entitled to sell protected seed to others under unusual circumstances.

Much discussion centered around the question of "minimum distance," i.e., how different must a new variety be from a derived parent to qualify for protection under variety protection laws. There was no agreement on this issue among conferees, but it was agreed that some quantifiable minimum genetic distance should be required for a variety to qualify for protection as a new entity.

Patenting of plant materials may interfere with exchange of materials among researchers and among government, university, and private laboratories. Such concerns could be allayed by a research exemption elective under utility patent law. Such an approach, however, would require revision of the patent law. An alternative approach would be for institutions desiring to provide a research exemption to adopt policies whereby an explicit research exemption is included in all licenses.

GERMPLASM AND INFORMATION EXCHANGE WORK GROUP

The goal of germplasm and information exchanges should be to make the best possible genetic resources available for use in solving world agricultural problems. Germplasm, broadly defined, includes all genetic materials and information associated with plants, such as landraces, advanced breeding lines, varieties, cloned genes, probes, nucleotide sequences, etc. Germplasm exchange ranges from very formal, with written and legally enforceable agreements, to informal exchange of materials between scientists with no exceptions or implied limitations on use of the materials.

Access to actual living plant materials, in the case of plant intellectual property, is more important than for other types of intellectual property. Higher plant germplasm is very difficult to describe verbally and impossible to duplicate simply from descriptions. Thus, improvement requires physical access to the germplasm itself, making exchanges extremely important to advancement of the science. Free exchange is understood to mean exchanges of an unrestricted nature, i.e., available to anyone, whereas *exchange for free* means that there are no costs associated with the exchange. "Exchange" also implies that each of two or more parties makes contributions to the transaction.

All germplasm has the potential to contain protectable intellectual property and any limitations on ownership or commercialization opportunities must be made clear by the owners. This is especially important for materials deposited in the world's gene banks. For example, the International Agriculture Research Centers (IARC) of the Consultative Group for International Agriculture Research (CGIAR) hold germplasm that is considered the property of the world's people. By institutional policy, it is available to all without restrictions. Moreover, it is expected that recipients will not subsequently protect any of the materials received from the IARCs and make any derived materials unavailable.

Work group members identified three important issues. First, scientist-to-scientist exchanges should be as unrestricted as possible and can be facilitated by (i) encouraging the use of research exemptions by all public institutions holding utility patents for plants, (ii) amending the U.S. Plant Variety Protection Act to provide protection against essentially derived varieties, and (iii) encouraging public institutions to adopt the same policies regarding availability of the products of molecular biology as for more traditional germplasm. Second, country-to-country exchanges should be unrestricted and freely available for distribution in small quantities to bona fide scientists for research purposes. Third, a mechanism is needed to preserve and distribute restricted-use germplasm. The group recommended convening a study panel to develop a system to ensure public availability of restricted material once statutory protection had expired.

The conferees recommended providing better information to students and scientists in agriculture regarding (i) intellectual property rights for plants, (ii) procedures for accessing genetic materials in gene banks, and (iii) situations where patents can either increase or decrease germplasm accessibility. The conferees also recommended providing information to administrators on the types of protection available and their implications for germplasm exchange.

SOCIAL AND ETHICAL ISSUES WORK GROUP

The social and ethical issues work group identified seven main questions with regard to intellectual property protection of plant materials. These include (i) which agencies, institutions, and individuals should have access to germplasm; (ii) what are the effects of intellectual property protection on biodiversity; (iii) should plant materials be considered private property; (iv) what are the effects of plant protection policies on the social structure of agriculture; (v) what is the impact of intellectual property policy on the sustainability, stability, and well being of the public sector research system; (vi) what rights should farmers retain after purchasing and growing protected seed; and (vii) what are the ethical considerations in educating the public and students about plant protection policies.

The following policies were recommended. (i) Educate students and the general public on the ethical dimensions of intellectual property issues. (ii)

Policy makers and legislators should consider consolidating intellectual property laws for plants to foster uniform protection for all types of plant intellectual property. (iii) A research exemption policy (e.g., uniform material transfer agreement) is essential for maximizing and facilitating breeder access to germplasm worldwide. This policy should apply to arrangements between private parties as well as those between private and public parties. (iv) An arbitration mechanism should be considered to resolve disputes on plant intellectual property. (v) Continued public and quasi-public funding of public sector research is essential to minimize the perceptions of impropriety stemming from direct relationships between public agencies and private companies. (vi) Policies should be developed to provide just compensation to developing nations for use of germplasm obtained from within their borders.

RESEARCH AGENDA WORK GROUP

Many universities are under pressure to seek research funds from non-traditional sources. Potential income from patent royalty is one such source. More importantly, however, in recent years the private sector has been willing to fund specific research projects at many universities. In providing this research funding, companies generally expect preferential access to intellectual property that might be developed. As part of their contractual obligation on grants, universities agree to seek appropriate protection for intellectual property. Similar obligations exist on federal grants.

The major impact of IPR on public sector research agendas is thus indirect. Because of public funding reductions, universities will undertake research for which external funds are available. Availability of external funds often depends on the ability of the institution to provide access to appropriately protected intellectual property. The opportunity for public institutions to receive income independently from royalty bearing licenses can also influence the choice of problems researchers undertake. Conferees agreed that adequate funding for high priority research from public sources would minimize the impact of IPR on the public sector research agenda.

As with the work group on exchanges, there was concern on the part of some work group members that property protection might restrict the exchange of germplasm and information. Other members believed that protection of intellectual property would encourage exchanges that might not otherwise occur. Some suggested that a research exemption in patent law similar to that in the PVPA would diminish the negative impact of protection on research agendas.

Work group members encouraged the development of concise educational and informational packages on intellectual property issues that could be used in discussions with policy makers and administrators. They also suggested that the PVPA be revised to conform to the 1991 UPOV Convention. Finally, work group members encouraged organizing forums to encourage public debate on the effects of patents, of state and federal funding, and of teaching demands on the research agenda.

OVERALL WORKSHOP RECOMMENDATIONS

A workshop synthesis group, consisting of work group chairs and rapporteurs, reviewed each work group's findings. The following are the five highest priority issues and recommended actions to address each of these issues.

Research Funding and Agenda Setting. Concerns about the impact of IPR on research agendas emanate primarily from the public sector. Continued erosion in state and federal funds for research has created pressures for university researchers to seek funds from other sources. Other sources include the private sector, from which funds can normally be secured much more readily if universities are willing to protect intellectual property and to grant licenses to sponsors of the research. Thus, the goals of long-term university funded specific projects or programs may be redirected (agenda modified) by the provider of the marginal funds needed to continue the program. This redirection of the research agenda is more directly related to funding than to intellectual property rights per se and is present regardless of whether the marginal funds are provided by a private sector entity or by a federal granting agency. The provider of the marginal funds has a very significant impact on the direction of the research program.

The prospect of direct royalty income from the licensing of intellectual property may also affect the research priorities at some institutions and with some individual researchers.

Recommendations. Decision makers should be better informed on the impact of intellectual property protection on shifts in the direction of research programs and the impact of such directional shifts on the ability of these programs to meet the public's expectations.

Effective efforts are needed to counteract the serious erosion of support for agricultural research in the public sector. Better public funding would mitigate the negative impact of IPR on public research agendas by removing much of the pressure to acquire marginal research money from the private sector where IPR must, by business necessity, be an important part of the funding arrangements.

Public institutions should improve their ability and capacity to manage intellectual property to encourage rapid commercial development while at the same time protecting the public interest.

Education and Communication. Decision makers and researchers generally lack adequate information about IPR and appropriate institutional procedures and policies for exercising these rights without compromising public interests.

Recommendations. Information about intellectual property issues should be published more widely, especially within the public agricultural research system.

Society's role and support for public sector agricultural research needs to be reassessed. Scientific literacy and recognition of the importance of science as part of agriculture need to be improved.

Model license and material transfer agreements should be developed and copies should be made available to intellectual property managers.

Farmer Exemptions. The farmer exemption of the PVPA, as it currently exists, weakens this form of protection to the point that it is of little value in many situations. Thus, utility patents are more widely sought than would be the case with a stronger variety protection law. Also, the current U.S. Act is inconsistent with the 1991 UPOV Convention.

Recommendation. The PVPA of 1970 should be revised to conform to 1991 UPOV regarding farmer exemptions and essentially derived varieties.

Germplasm Exchanges and Research Exemptions. Exchange of breeding and research materials among scientists is essential for continued progress in plant improvement. Intellectual property protection should not interfere with such exchanges.

Recommendations. An explicit research exemption should be provided with utility patents on plants. In the absence of such an exemption, public institutions should be encouraged to grant a research exemption as an integral part of their institutional licensing policy.

Deposits of all biological materials required for IPR should become part of the national germplasm system.

International Considerations. The international dimensions of IPR, including compensation to third world countries, continue to be a source of contention among scientists.

Recommendations. Developing countries should be encouraged to adopt effective plant breeders rights and intellectual property laws.

Country-to-country plant germplasm exchanges should be encouraged by whatever means appropriate.

Equity issues in germplasm exchanges, including compensation to countries of origin, should be addressed and appropriate steps taken to assure that exchanges are unfettered.

1 Introduction: Intellectual Property Rights Workshop

John H. Barton

Stanford Law School
Stanford University
Stanford, CA

This paper provides a short review of intellectual property law for those unfamiliar with the area and points out certain important issues for special consideration. Of these issues, the most important is the growing extension of intellectual property rights into earlier and earlier phases of the research and development process.

INTELLECTUAL PROPERTY BACKGROUND AND IMPORTANT LEGAL DEVELOPMENTS SINCE THE 1989 WORKSHOP

Plant Breeder's Rights

Plant Breeder's Rights or Plant Variety Protection provides a minimum form of protection adapted to the needs of the traditional breeder. It protects against resale (with certain limited exceptions) of the seed of a protected variety, but permits use of that seed as a parent for future breeding. The approach thus respects the breeders' traditional reliance on heavy interchange of material and on building on one another's advances.

In 1991, the basic international treaty defining this form of protection, the International Union for the Protection of New Varieties of Plants (UPOV) Convention, was amended. Those amendments will have no formal impact until they are accepted by national governments and converted into national law; nevertheless, they give us a good sense of what is coming. The new UPOV Convention includes two particularly important changes. The first may limit the farmer's privilege. As I implied above, under current law, farmers are free to use their harvest as seed; in addition, under the U.S. variant of the law, farmers can resell a certain amount as seed. The new UPOV Convention would create a norm that farmers no longer have these rights—but would permit national governments to create such an exemption if they choose.

The second change involves a new concept of an ''essentially derived variety.'' Although this concept serves other purposes as well, its intent can most readily be seen in the context of biotechnology. Suppose a biotechnologist inserts a new gene into a variety protected under Plant Breeder's Rights. Under current law, the breeder who had spent much time and energy creating that variety would have no rights over the modified variety, and the inserter of the new gene could assert complete rights. That seems inequitable. Hence, the new concept ensures that a holder of Plant Breeder's Rights protection can assert rights over a variety that differs only slightly from the protected variety. The biotechnologist and the original breeder, in this example, are both likely to have the right to keep the ''essentially derived variety'' off the market; the result will be strong incentives for a reasonable compromise.

Regular Patent Rights

Since the American Society of Agronomy's last discussion of these issues at its 1989 Workshop (Caldwell & Schillinger, 1989), there have been important evolutions in the application of the regular patent system to agriculture; this patent system is likely to prove of enormous importance in the future. This patent system is, of course, the system under which utility, novelty, and non-obviousness have to be shown, and a disclosure to the patent office has to be made.

Along with patents on a variety of processes, two kinds of patents are emerging as having substantial significance for agricultural breeding. The first kind includes patents on a new variety. A number of private sector breeders are obtaining regular patent protection for their marketed varieties or on their inbred parental lines. Such patents are clearly intended to serve much the same function as would Plant Breeder's Rights protection. Although the patent office is granting the patents, there has not yet been a court decision on whether this application of the patent law should be foreclosed by the more specific Plant Breeder's Rights law. If the patents are valid, they may have greater effective force than the Plant Breeder's Rights certificate. They would probably be interpreted, for example, as permitting no farmer's privilege. Moreover, the use of the patented materials in breeding would be permissible only within the scope of the experimental use exemption; this exemption is much more narrow and less clear than its Plant Breeder's Rights analogue.

The other form of patent, which is almost certainly generally valid, is the patent on a gene. I want to emphasize exactly what is meant by patenting a gene. The patent application in such a situation typically discloses the sequence of the gene, and then typically claims first, a gene or protein, standing alone, corresponding to that sequence; second, a vector or plasmid incorporating the sequence; and, possibly, third, a plant (of a particular range of species) that has been transformed by means of such a vector (and the descendents of the transformed plant). Thus, the patent holder gains effective control over use of the specified gene in genetic engineering. If however, the same gene is found naturally in a species, a breeder can use traditional breeding techniques to include the gene in a cultivar without infringing the patent.

Two current controversies in the patent area also deserve attention. The first is the first-to-file versus first-to-invent controversy associated with the proposed Patent Harmonization Treaty. Although the exact future of this treaty is mixed with that of the intellectual property component of the Uruguay Round of trade negotiations, there is a good probability that within the next several years, we will shift to the first-to-file system.

What this means is exemplified by the situation of two inventors, who make the same invention, independently, but file at different times. Very possibly, the first to invent will not be the first to file. In the USA—and one other nation, the Philippines—the patent office or court attempts to reconstruct the actual order in which the firms made the invention. In a typical biotechnology context, this effort may require extremely expensive litigation. There are frequently separate steps of purification, assay, probe development, sequence identification, actual sequencing, and possibly synthesis—and several firms may be competing in this process, with different firms leading at different steps. Under the first-to-file system, the first one to the patent office automatically wins.

Very likely, this change will be accompanied by other changes. Thus, in the U.S. system, in a pattern that universities like, one can publish and still file for a patent within a year; elsewhere there is no such grace period. And, in most nations, unlike the USA, patents are made public at a fixed time, typically 18 months after filing, even before they have been granted. We will almost certainly have a compromise in which we adapt first-to-file and some form of early publication. There is the chance for inequitable results under the first-to-file arrangement; the net litigation cost of the alternative probably outweighs this potential inequity.

The other important development is the controversy surrounding the National Institute of Health's (NIH) application for a patent on certain human genome sequences. Dr. Craig Venter at the NIH developed a procedure for identifying and rapidly sequencing portions of the genes being expressed in a specific tissue. What he obtained were sequences for a component of a gene, not a whole gene. NIH applied for a patent on these sequences; its application has been initially rejected, but this is not yet a decisive resolution.

As a matter of law, the patent application raises a number of questions, primarily going to novelty, obviousness, and utility. The concerns about novelty and utility arose from the facts that some of the sequences were not new, that it was believed easy to obtain a whole gene from a partial sequence, and that the materials used were derived from a publicly available complementary-DNA library. The utility issue is the more interesting one. The patent application claimed use of these fragments for developing probes to identify the entire sequences. This claim, in which the invention helps one in the research stage, is very similar to claims rejected in a 1966 Supreme Court patent case, *Brenner* v. *Manson*, 383 U.S. 519 (1966), which held that the invention had to offer ''specific benefit. . . in currently available form.'' I would find the Supreme Court decision decisive—but, at the lower court level and potentially at the Supreme Court level as well, the doctrine has evolved substantially since 1966.

One point to note in particular about this application is that the NIH may have been concerned about ensuring the commercial development potential for the various proteins on which it had identified partial sequences. The reasoning was that the identification of a sequence has traditionally been the decisive point for patentability—this is not a statement of formal legal doctrine but an empirical description of how courts actually behave. This choice of a decisive point worked well in the old days in which one began with a candidate ''factor x'' with a particular biological impact, and ultimately found the sequence for that factor. With the genome project, however, we will, sooner or later, start with sequences and attempt to find out what the coded protein is good for. Is there a new point of patentability? If not—or if we determine that the publication of the sequence for the entire human genome undercuts novelty for any included gene—no patent may be available. If so, will a firm have the incentive to invest the funds necessary to bring a product to market on the basis of the relevant sequence?

IMPORTANT U.S. ISSUES

The NIH patent application, although currently unsuccessful, reflects a contemporary trend to assert intellectual property rights earlier and earlier in the research process. This is partly a result of changes in biotechnology and in patent law. It is partly also a result of the sense, enshrined in the Bayh-Dole Act, 35 U.S.C. §§ 200-210, and Stevenson-Wydler Act, 15 U.S.C. §§ 3701-14, that universities and government laboratories can contribute to national competitiveness if they patent their developments and license the patents. (I am not at all sure that this is an accurate judgment or if we would do better to put these inventions in the public domain). The trend also reflects the fact that universities and other research institutions see the possibility of profit in commercial applications of their technology. They therefore seek to protect a right to bargain for a portion of the profits from downstream inventions that depend on their own inventions.

Examples are manifold and go well beyond the human genome issue itself. Thus, I understand that, in Europe, there are patent applications filed on receptors, based on the sequences of these receptors. The intent is presumably that, by being the first to clone and identify the receptor, one can claim the right to use artificial versions of that receptor in drug identification and evaluation. The patent holder would thus effectively carve out a claim over any therapeutic procedures developed for the diseases relevant to that receptor, assuming that the therapy is based on studies using artifically produced versions of the receptor. Similarly, I'm familiar with another U.S. patent with claims on certain compositions of stem cells (the precursors of the immune system cells), U.S. Patent 5,061,620, October 29, 1991. Potentially, such a patent affects a wide area of immunological or genetic therapy.

The courts have a number of rules, whose current application is not yet clear, for dealing with such patents. Traditionally, no patent could be granted on a law of nature. The legal argument was that such a patent would preempt too much science; as the Brenner Court put it, such a patent could "confer power to block off whole areas of scientific development, without compensating benefit to public." Perhaps the underlying policy argument issue is that the academic grant and publishing process may be more effective here, just as the patent and investment process is sometimes more effective when a product is close to commercialization. Similarly, the utility rule prohibits patents that are sought on an invention that is too far from possible application to an actual product. And the experimental use exemption presumably permits some use of a patented invention during research—although it has typically been read as permitting only purely academic, non-commercial research.

This movement toward intellectual property protection of early research results is paralleled by trends in material transfer agreements—the agreements which most universities now require their researchers to require as part of transferring any genetic material to other researchers. Typically, in addition to provisions designed to disclaim any possible liabilities, the provisions of these agreements require the recipient to use the material for research purposes only and not to transfer it to third parties. Most important, if a commercial invention derives from the recipient's use, the recipient is committed to negotiate with the supplier about sharing the profits. These agreements have become more and more common; the legal offices of universities will typically require their use.

The profit-sharing provisions can help bring windfall profits into the public sector. They can also be tricky and we've had little experience in actually implementing the sharing that is to occur when profits finally do arise. If, on the one hand, the agreement simply specifies a duty to negotiate, the negotiation itself may prove unworkable—suppose there is a such a duty with respect to 16 parents of a marketed variety! Similarly, a pre-specified royalty can present problems—suppose (as is, in fact, unlikely) all 16 parents had been promised a 6% royalty. Perhaps worst of all, what if some research inputs have been promised a fixed royalty and others a duty to negotiate?

THE BIODIVERSITY CONVENTION

Turning to the international level, one of the most important movements toward earlier protection is that implicit in the Convention on Biological Diversity. This is one of the Conventions that was negotiated at the Rio de Janeiro Conference on the Environment and Development last spring. The USA refused to sign, in large part because of certain intellectual property issues, but most analysts believe that the new Clinton administration will adhere to the Convention.

The Convention contains a number of provisions requiring parties to create biological reserves and carry out a variety of other measures intended to protect their biological diversity. These provisions are, however, quite weak. Stronger proposals, including development of a world priority list of important conservation regions or of important endangered species, were rejected in the preliminary negotiations at Nairobi. The intellectual property issues included carefully hedged and somewhat confusing obligations to transfer technology relevant to conserving and using genetic resources. The provisions were in fact much weaker than their U.S. critics argued.

The provisions of most importance to agriculture were those recognizing national sovereignty over genetic resources. The Convention rejects the whole idea of free flow of genetic resources, i.e., the common heritage concept. The implication is that any future collector of genetic materials will have to sign the equivalent of a material transfer agreement, and presumably agree to track the uses of the material and to ensure that the donor nation receives a share of any profits that may emerge from the material. By the terms of the Convention, this national sovereignty concept applies only to material newly collected in the future, and does not apply to material now in genebanks, but there are proposals for efforts to define source-nation rights over materials in genebanks.

In the belief that the evolution of these principles is extremely important to the future of global and U.S. agriculture, the new National Genetic Resources Advisory Council has asked the incoming Secretary of Agriculture to ensure that agriculture's concerns are raised in the new administration's deliberations over adeherence to the Biodiversity Convention.

TOWARD THE FUTURE

This analysis defines what I believe should be the agenda for those in U.S. agriculture who are interested in intellectual property issues.

1. What can be done—almost certainly in the strictly legal or legislative communities—to ensure the development of doctrines to restrict the movement of intellectual property rights to points very early in the research process? Might, for example, existing proposals for codifica-

tion of the research exemption be helpful? Should utility be similarly codified?

2. What can be done about overly extensive material transfer agreements? The NIH is developing a model agreement for use by its grantees; the model, of course, attempts a reasonable balance of interests. Might a similar effort be useful in agriculture?
3. What about the Biodiversity Convention? Is it possible to negotiate a uniform material transfer agreement with developing nations that deals fairly with the issue? What about the possibility of excluding agriculture, on the grounds that the larger profits are in the medicinal area and that the industrial structure is there much more conducive to a property right on behalf of developing nations? Is there a way that the administration can safeguard agriculture's position in signing the Convention?

REFERENCES

Caldwell, B.E., and J.A. Schillinger (ed.). 1989. Intellectual property rights associated with plants. ASA Spec. Publ. 52. CSSA, ASA, and SSSA, Madison, WI.

2 Goals and Expectations of Industry for Intellectual Property Rights for Plant Materials

Donald N. Duvick

6837 N.W. Beaver Drive
Johnston, IA

The term ''industry working with plant materials'' includes a variety of commercial enterprises that are concerned with plants in one way or another. This discussion will deal primarily with research-based seed companies, and companies that produce novel genotypes (usually through biotechnology) for use in plant breeding. Although university and government sectors also now look to making profits from plant manipulations, this paper will speak for those institutions that depend completely on profits for their existence—traditional full-time businesses.

GOALS—PROPRIETARY PRODUCTS AND PROFITABILITY

Industry's goals seemingly are simple. Each company in the plant genetic supply industry seeks to develop unique products, clearly superior to those of the competition. Such products will be preferred by the market, by the customers. If the products also can be produced and sold economically, the company with the best products will be financially successful.

Companies therefore need to protect their innovations–the products of their investment in research–from unrestricted use by others. But they also want to use innovations from elsewhere–innovations that have been developed by other individuals and other organizations. These twin goals may seem to present an impossible contradiction, but they merely point out that industry needs and wants well-defined rules of the game. Companies need industry-wide rules that allow owners to set out terms of use for their products, and also rules that make it clear how and when products from elsewhere can be used.

MONOPOLIES

The word ''monopoly'' is frequently used in reference to intellectual property protection for plants; e.g., patents are described as temporary, limited monopolies. Sometimes the word is used in the expression, ''monopoly profits,'' which seems to imply that monopolies always ensure profits, perhaps unfairly high profits. This conclusion is not true. Profits are not a necessary consequence of monopoly.

The term, monopoly, commonly is used in more than one sense. Definitions of monopoly can range from exclusive control of an irreplaceable commodity or service in a particular market, down to simple exclusive possession or control of a unique but not irreplaceable piece of property.

With the first kind of monopoly, sometimes called ''a true monopoly,'' there is the opportunity to set prices, regardless of the usual supply and demand forces. With the second type, at the other end of the scale, market forces are the predominant lever for setting prices and determining profitability.

Intellectual property protection for plants, exclusive ownership of some aspect of plants, tends to be on materials that are at neither end of this continuum. Owners cannot set prices with complete independence because their properties can be replaced by similar ones in the hands of others, but on the other hand, owners can prohibit others from using (selling) their protected products and so have an exclusive right to market those unique products as best they can.

Thus, the ability to own intellectual property (and rules regarding such ownership) do not give unlimited power to the plant genetic supply industry, but nevertheless they are needed and helpful. One should note that intellectual property rights are useful not only to sequester, but also to distribute germplasm and ideas. Both actions are needed by industry, as well as by others concerned with plant breeding.

INDUSTRY NEEDS GERMPLASM EXCHANGE

The commercial plant breeding industry, including companies that aim to supply useful new genotypes to plant breeders for a price, requires a constant infusion of new genotypes, and new ideas about how to use them to make desired new varieties and/or plant parts and products. No one company, even the largest, can hope to provide all the genotypes, all the knowledge it will need to turn out superior products. Public institutions are invaluable sources of germplasm and knowledge, but they can no longer satisfy all the needs of today's increasingly knowledge-based seed industry.

Pure necessity, therefore, leads competitors to deal with each other from time to time, to exchange materials and knowledge on mutually acceptable terms. The hope of each company is that it can do better than its competitors in using the new materials and ideas to turn out proprietary products. The concept is not very different from that of trading players among baseball clubs, each club hoping to get in trades what it needs to build a superior, proprietary product–a championship team.

Thus, each plant materials company wants control over its products (its finished varieties, its reconstructed genes or its new process descriptions) based on property rights, and at the same time, it wants to be able to go to the market place and in an orderly and ethical fashion obtain access to certain properties that its competitors or other institutions and individuals are willing to trade or sell or license. Intellectual property rights are used to assist companies in achieving both of these goals. They are used not only to prevent unauthorized use of proprietary products but also to give increased accessibility to them, when appropriate. Restricted access means not only sequestration but also licensing.

GOALS—LEGAL ASSISTANCE IN GERMPLASM UTILIZATION

To state these concepts of intellectual property protection for plants is relatively easy. To implement them is more difficult. The history of the U.S. Plant Patent Act, the International Union for the Protection of New Varieties of Plants (UPOV), the U.S. Plant Variety Protection Act (PVPA), applications of utility patents to plants, and utilization of trade secrets, testifies to the many ways in which commercial interests have attempted to improve their ability to profit from investments in plant research (Lesser, 1991). Development of the ''Farmers' Rights'' concept among some third world countries also has been an attempt to find ways of giving a measure of profitability to those in the developing countries that have in hand diverse and potentially useful supplies of plant germplasm (FAO, 1989; RAFI, 1989).

None of the methods devised, to date, has been as successful as its sponsors had hoped. However, neither have they caused as many problems as their detractors predicted. For it must be said, that nearly all of the initiatives in intellectual property rights for plants have raised fears, particularly in recent years, among specific special interest groups.

CONCERNS ABOUT INTELLECTUAL PROPERTY RIGHTS

The fears are as diverse as the backgrounds of the concerned groups (Caldwell & Schillinger, 1989; Belcher & Hawtin, 1991; Fowler & Mooney, 1990; Keystone, 1991; Kloppenberg, 1987; OTA, 1989). Small seed companies have feared that utility patents, especially as used with biotechnology products, would force them out of business. Third world countries and sympathizing social action organizations have feared that intellectual property protection on plants would deprive third world farmers, at least the smaller ones, of everyday sources of germplasm for their farmer-scale selection and breeding. First world farmers have feared that plant variety protection would deprive them of the freedom to save and replant seed from their own commercial crop, or to sell some of it to others as occasion presents itself. Traditional plant breeders have feared that patents on genes and other genetic products of biotechnology would deprive them of sources of germplasm for classical recombination and breeding. People and organizations concerned with crop genetic diversity per se have feared that intellectual property protection on plants would lock up germplasm in private hands, thereby reducing the effective size of the germplasm base available for publicly-supported breeding. Commercial breeders have feared that public institutions, eager to profit from their research, would restrictively license their protected products to only a few companies, thus depriving other firms of the results of tax-financed research.

Briefly, each attempt to increase protection for research products of a particular group has raised fears among other groups that the exchange and availability of germplasm would be curtailed to their disadvantage.

Industry needs to do its part to find answers to the questions of concerned groups and individuals, to help identify those fears that are based on fact, and then to help make adjustments that remove or alleviate the problems. To do so will help industry in the long run, as well as helping the concerned special interest groups. And of course if investigation shows that certain fears are unfounded, industry aided by public interest groups can inform and educate the public about such new knowledge, also to the advantage of all concerned parties.

UTILITY PATENTS AND GERMPLASM EXCHANGE

During the past several years in the USA, attention has been turned to uses of utility patents for protection of plant varieties as well as for protection of products of biotechnology applied to plants (ASA, 1989; OTA, 1989). Patents for biotechnology inventions have seemed a natural extension of patents for chemical inventions. Patents for plant varieties seemed to be a less obvious need until problems arose with unauthorized large-scale sales of varieties protected under PVPA, or with unauthorized use of materials treated as trade secrets. Utility patents were considered as capable of giving added protection in both of these areas. This extra protection from utility patents is not looked on with favor by all, however.

For example, plant variety protection automatically allows use of protected varieties for further breeding, the so-called ''Research (or Breeders') Exemption,'' but U.S. utility patents do not give this permission automatically (OTA 1989). It is dependent upon the decision of the owner of the property.

Thus, unless authorized, one cannot use the patent-protected property of others for development of new commercial varieties.

Ability to prevent others from using patented varieties for development of new ones has been cited as potentially leading to additional, and unacceptable, narrowing of an already too narrow germplasm base. But this conclusion seems to be unwarranted for the following reasons.

Without the possibility of patent protection, private investment in certain kinds of research would be curtailed or absent. As a consequence, certain kinds of privately developed germplasm would not be invented and so would be available to no one. If invented and patented, they would be available to the patent holder and perhaps to licensees, for productive use by farmers. Such invention and use would broaden, not narrow, the total active germplasm base.

Licensing, as just noted, can be used to increase the availability of patented germplasm. Some developers have this end in mind, as the chief way they plan to profit from investment in research and development. And although some inventions are not intended for license, at expiration of patent protection they will be available for research and use without restriction.

It also is likely that relatively few plant varieties will be patented, compared to the number that receive plant variety protection. Requirements for patenting are more stringent than those for plant variety protection; e.g., a clear-cut inventive step is required for patent eligibility, as compared to the simpler requirement of "distinctiveness", for plant variety protection.

One also must remember that trade secret protection has been and still is used, to sequester certain kinds of germplasm from use by others. In theory, such protection can last forever. Absence of patent protection would not remove the ability to keep privately owned germplasm a trade secret; indeed, the method was used many years before either plant variety protection or utility patents were available to plant breeders in the USA.

Finally, there are conflicting forces at work, some of which tend to ensure a broad germplasm base. Thus, if a company is foreclosed by patents from using a competitor's property to develop new varieties (foreclosed from breeding in the competitor's genetic base), its breeders may find it necessary to look for new sources of genes and genetic variation and thus expand the genetic base used by the industry as a whole. If they are successful, the company also will protect the new property it has developed and again will push the industry to seek still other new sources of genes and variation.

Despite these reasons for believing that utility patents on varieties, genes, and other genetic materials will not unduly restrict their use in further breeding, a prudent approach for industry will be to continue to look into possible problems in this regard, with intention to correct any that unreasonably restrict useful and timely exchange of germplasm for breeding. The intention would be, to continually improve the effectiveness of intellectual property rights in promoting germplasm use and exchange.

FURTHER NEEDS AND EXPECTATIONS

Extensive experience with plant variety protection and initial experience with utility patents indicates that intellectual property protection alone cannot guarantee needed controls over proprietary products of research, nor can it guarantee a profitable business. Nevertheless, it also is clear that the genetic supply industry will need to use both kinds of intellectual property protection as appropriate, to supplement the more fundamental actions of creative and efficient research, economic and reliable production, and enthusiastic and effective sales operations.

Future expectations of industry in regard to intellectual property protection for plant materials are in at least two areas: plant variety protection and utility patents.

With regard to plant variety protection, industry hopes to have tighter legal controls over unauthorized reproduction and sale of its protected varieties. Such practices or the prospect of them have discouraged industry's entry into some crops, and have actually driven industry out of business after it had entered the market, in other crops. Storm-proof cotton, hard red winter wheat, and hard red spring wheat are crops in which unauthorized, wide-spread production and sale of seed of protected varieties has caused some companies to stop their research-based seed operations, even though they had made considerable investments in research and had made good progress in development of improved varieties.

Industry also hopes to see improvements in appreciation and knowledge of utility patents for products of biotechnology and other kinds of precise genetic manipulation. Such improved understanding is needed in government and academia, as well as in industry. On the one hand, clarification is needed on scope of protection. Patents with unreasonably broad protection either inhibit further research to solve a particular need, or they bring on protracted and expensive lawsuits. Sometimes both consequences ensue. On the other hand, lack of knowledge of scope and kinds of protection available with patents leads inventors to be unduly secretive and unwilling to share genetic materials and ideas, even though they could do so without losing proprietary rights. This causes unnecessary slowness in advancing knowledge through research.

Perhaps the greatest needs, not just for industry, but for all concerned are to (i) clearly delineate the advantages of intellectual property protection, not only for sequestration, but also for sharing of genetic materials and ideas pertaining to them; and (ii) to identify the present and/or potential problems and disadvantages in use of intellectual property protection for plants, especially in regard to genetic diversity. This should be done with the intention of facilitating correction or amelioration of the problems.

CONCLUSIONS

Industry's goal is to increase the rate and amount of useful germplasm exchange from breeders to farmers, and to do so by using the spur of market competition. For plant genetic supply companies to operate successfully, competitively, and ethically, proprietary rights to germplasm are necessary. Such rights need to be clearly delineated and broadly observed. Intellectual property rights on germplasm will assist in achievement of this goal. It is understood that intellectual property rights can serve and will be used by public as well as private interests, that to institute the system in areas where it has never existed before will entail problems and adjustments, and that intellectual property rights alone cannot solve needs of industry to be profitable, competitive, and socially useful.

REFERENCES

Caldwell, B.E., and J.A. Schillinger (ed.). 1989. Intellectual property rights assoicated with plants. ASA Spec. Publ. 52. CSSA, ASA, and SSSA, Madison, WI.

Belcher, B., and G. Hawtin. 1991. Patent on life: Ownership of plant and animal research. IDRC, Ottawa.

Food and Agriculture Organization of the United Nations. 1989. Report: Commission on plant genetic resources, 3rd session, p. 12–14. Rome. 17–21 April 1989. FAO, Rome.

Fowler, C., and P. Mooney. 1990. Shattering—Food, Politics, and the Loss of Genetic Diversity. Univ. of Arizona Press, Tucson.

Keystone. 1991. Final consensus report: Global initiative for the security and sustainable use of plant genetic resources, 3rd Plenary Session. *In* Keystone Intl Dialogue Series on Plant Genetic Resources, Oslo, Norway. 31 May–4 June 1991. The Keystone Center, Keystone, CO.

Kloppenburg, J. 1987. First the seed: The political economy of plant biotechnology, 1492–2000. Cambridge University Press, New York.

Lesser, W. 1991. Equitable patent protection in the developing world: Issues and approaches. Eubios Ethics Inst., Christchurch, New Zealand.

Office of Technology Assessment. 1989. New developments in biotechnology: Patenting life—Special Report. U.S. Congress, Office of Technology Assessment, OTA-BA-370. U.S. Gov. Print. Office, Washington, DC.

Rural Advancement Fund International Communique. 1989. Farmers' rights: The informal innovation system at GATT (TRIPS) & in intellectual property negotiations in the context of new biotechnologies. RAFI, Pittsboro, NC.

3 Expectations of Inventors, Owners, and Users—A University Perspective

Richard L. Lower

University of Wisconsin-Madison
Madison, WI

From a public university perspective, the following questions can be posed with respect to the expectations of inventors, owners, and users of intellectual property protection of plant materials.

1. What do inventors and owners expect to accomplish when seeking intellectual property protection of plants and plant derived materials? Why do they seek protection—whether it be protection under utility patent, plant variety protection, or plant patent laws?
2. Has the motivation to protect plant materials and the benefits expected from property protection changed in the last several years? If so, how?
3. What are the responsibilities and expectations of potential users of protected plant material? What latitude should be allowed for the use of protected plant material for further research purposes?
4. What do you expect in the future with regard to benefits and expectations of property protection?

In responding to these questions, the collective views of experiment station and land-grant university administrators should be represented to the extent possible. Certainly, this is a formidable challenge.

Before addressing these specific topics and charges, a brief historical perspective is appropriate. Public germplasm research has been conducted for over a century and is a primary responsibility of the State Agricultural Experiment Stations (SAES). The successes of SAES include cooperation with other public agencies as well as private industry in germplasm research. Much of this success can be attributed to (i) the free exchange of information as well as the free exchange of germplasm; and (ii) the development of a cooperative infrastructure that allows new germplasm to be acquired, maintained, shared,

 Intellectual Property Rights: Protection of Plant Materials, CSSA Special Publication no. 21.

developed, enhanced, and ultimately accepted by science and commerce. Part of the SAES/university responsibilities are to contribute directly to the training and education of geneticists, plant breeders, biotechnologists, and other plant scientists. Many believe this is their primary mission. This human resource pool is accompanied by an improved germplasm pool, new technology, breeding methodology, and sometimes cultivars as products of their mission.

The SAESs also respond to other rather common situations. In some states, a lack or paucity of acceptable private varieties because of a unique production or marketing opportunity has resulted in development of publicly supported germplasm programs and the release of public cultivars. Small acreage specialty crops of major economic importance to a state, but with little interest or incentive to private firms, also are supported by SAES programs.

It is appropriate to make a few comments about the environment in which agricultural experiment stations and land-grant universities operate today. University and agriculture experiment station budgets are extremely tight. The costs of doing research are escalating rapidly and there are increased pressures on the funding base. University budgets are becoming more student-driven and there are increased demands on faculty for instruction. Universities are hiring more discipline-oriented scientists and they rely more heavily on grants and contracts, both public and private, for support as state contributions make up a smaller portion of our budgets. Stronger university-industry relationships and greater dependence on revenues generated via intellectual property rights (IPR) are being considered as significant sources of research support.

At the same time, higher education is frequently perceived as aloof, detached, and nonresponsive to public needs. The charges of conflict of interest and abuse of indirect cost returns have contributed to an image problem nationally. Issues and problems at land-grant universities are increasingly complex and they are operating under a stricter regulatory environment with increasing demands for accountability. Yet, the opportunities for progress have never been better. The human resource pool available today is well trained, eager to learn, and dedicated to improving the quality of life.

Over the past 18 months, numerous national and international activities have magnified the importance of IPR and they complicate and energize the workshop agenda. The Biodiversity Convention (Article 15) and the International Undertaking by the Food and Agriculture Organization of the United Nations (FAO) are addressing the sovereign rights of natural resources. The 1991 International Union for the Protection of New Varieties of Plants (UPOV) Convention espouses limited use of farm saved seed and the concept of essentially derived varieties. The Food and Drug Administration's (FDA) ruling on products of biotechnology and the National Institutes of Health (NIH) request to patent 2750 partial complementary-DNA sequences of unknown function are also impacting germplasm programs. The General Agreement on Tariff and Trade (GATT), the North American Free Trade Act

(NAFTA), and the debate/potential change in the U.S. patent system from a first-to-discover (invent) to a first-to-file system also are examples of activities that heighten the need for this workshop.

In addressing specific topics, one should remember that researchers at agricultural experiment stations make two major contributions to science: (i) creating knowledge (via their research from the molecular level to the site of application); and (ii) training and developing the human resource.

Question 1. What do scientists expect to accomplish and why do they seek intellectual property protection for plant germplasm?

Recognition of research accomplishments and accountability are extremely important in today's world. Germplasm protection, regardless of the type, [i.e., plant variety protection (PVP), utility patent, plant patent, or some form of license] is a form of recognition and reward for the conduct of quality research. This recognition is important to morale and in many cases to the tenure, promotion, and merit processes as well.

IPR provides a form of protection of our economic interest. In some instances, this may be with the intent of developing or preserving funding sources needed to keep research programs viable.

Question 2. What is the motivation and/or the benefit of IPR?

The public, as well as university governing bodies, expect products of tax-dollar supported research to be protected. After all, compensation for research accomplishments is one way to support future endeavors. Until the 1980s, public universities and agricultural experiment stations usually gave things away. They were available as public domain. Many say this was right, since most germplasm research was funded by state and federal formula dollars. Scientists participated in research and exchanged materials openly (although this is a bit of a myth) and with few, if any, restrictions.

Today the motivation to protect germplasm has increased. Tighter university budgets have redirected administrators and researchers to think more carefully about cost containment and cost recovery. Some sort of royalty recovery is desirable to support germplasm programs. Germplasm exchanges are still taking place, but are frequently accompanied by memoranda of understanding or memoranda of agreements that place limits or restrictions on the usage of the germplasm. the legal profession calls these material transfer agreements. Germplasm transactions are more frequently accompanied by this kind of paperwork today. It is hoped that germplasm research programs are not being directed with the sole intent of making dollars or generating support via royalty from releases. This is a treadmill that should be avoided. Base support for university germplasm programs should not be solely dependent on patents or revenue derived from intellectual property protection. Remember, the biggest contribution and primary mission of universities is the training of students—human resources development.

Question 3. What are the responsibilities and expectations regarding use of protected germplasm?

The present Experiment Station Committee on Organization and Policy (ESCOP) guidelines are clear about the use of protected plant material. They allow for and recommend protection in order to recognize accomplishment and ownership. At the same time, they advocate that protected public germplasm be available as "state-of-the-art" breeding material to bona fide breeders who request it. An exemption from seeking approval for research use ("a research clause") is recommended. Further, there are suggested mechanisms that allow recompense to the initial inventor when a new germplasm development is released that utilizes the initial protected germplasm and is competitive with the initial inventor's property. These guidelines also allow for individual agricultural experiment stations to respond to situations unique to their states and still participate in germplasm improvement and exchanges and to contribute to state, national, and international food and fiber industries. After all, success in developing food and fiber germplasm has been based on the sharing of genetic resources.

Question 4. What do we expect in the future regarding IPR?

The future will be exciting, demanding, and full of opportunities. The traditional breeding methodologies in combination with the emerging molecular technologies will lead to development of new and improved germplasm. Random amplified polymorphic DNA (RAPD), restriction fragment length polymorphism (RFLP), and polymerase chain reaction (PCR) technologies will also allow for accurate and positive identification of germplasm. These molecular techniques will be important to germplasm identification, determination of rightful ownership, and enforcement of patent rights. Modern biology is moving at a rapid rate and the legal system will be challenged to cope with the changes on both national and international scenes. Protection should become easier rather than more difficult.

Lastly, dollars to support germplasm research that is not directly profit oriented will continue to be short. The U.S. germplasm pool is the envy of the world. The lack of support to enhance germplasm collections is critical to the conduct of research. The newly formed National Genetic Resources Advisory Council offers hope in the form of solid national leadership and the prospect of research support for this vast quantity of germplasm. Ethical issues and conflict of interest issues will challenge land-grant institutions at every turn through the 1990s.

4 Intellectual Property Protection of Plants—The Agricultural Research Service Perspective

R. D. Plowman

U.S. Department of Agriculture
Agricultural Research Service
Washington, DC

Plant breeders can be justifiably proud of the accomplishments they have made over the past 40 years. All of the major agricultural crops show large increases in yield. One has only to plot increased yields over years to gain an appreciation of the steady growth that has occurred. It is no wonder that the USA has fewer farmers to feed our people than any other country in the world. Recent estimates show that only 2% of the people produce the food and fiber to take care of our needs and have additional produce to export. American agriculture is a great success story.

While it is true that not all of the productivity gains can be attributed to genetic improvement, much of the progress we have made in crops such as wheat, corn, oats, barley, rice, alfalfa, clover, grasses, and cotton has come as a result of breeding.

Of course, great strides have been made in enhancing cultural practices during this same period and such improvements have helped increase yields. But conservative estimates attribute more than 60% of yield increases during the last four decades to improvements through breeding.

In all of these crops, there have been both private and public breeders who have dedicated careers to the continuous development of new varieties.

The creation of these new varieties has played a major role through the years in helping U.S. farmers maintain their economic viability. In corn alone, average yields have increased from 39.7 bushels per acre in 1950 to 106.5 bushels per acre in 1990—a total increase of 168.3%. Similarly, wheat yields have risen from 16.5 bushels per acre in 1950 to 35.4 bushels per acre just 40 years later, in 1990—a 114.5% increase (Table 1–1).

If farmers were dependent today on the increases due only to cultivation improvements, they would not be able to survive in the current economic times. Overall production costs have risen, so it has become essential to the

 Intellectual Property Rights: Protection of Plant Materials, CSSA Special Publication no. 21.

Table 1–1. Three-year average yield of major U.S. agricultural crops, 1950–1990.

Crop	Years					Percent increase over 40 years
	1950	1960	1970	1980	1990	
Corn, bu/A	39.7	52.1	79.3	100.5	106.5	168.3
Potato, cwt/A	139.6	185.3	221.3	268.0	287.3	105.8
Wheat, Bu/A	16.5	25.1	30.0	33.0	35.4	114.5
Oats, bu/A	35.0	40.1	51.9	53.2	51.2	46.3
Barley, bu/A	25.8	29.6	43.5	49.9	47.5	84.1
Rice, lb/A	2242	3323	4435	4499	5590	149.3
Cotton, lb/A	288.1	457.7	462.7	457.0	624.3	116.7
Soybeans, bu/A	21.9	23.7	27.0	29.3	31.1	42.0
Alfalfa, tons/A	2.25	2.25	2.76	3.09	2.96	31.6

competitiveness and economic viability of our farmers that cost per unit of yield decrease.

Genetic progress and development of new varieties is not just a domestic issue. International needs for food and fiber have continued to grow. In the past 40 years, the world's population has risen from 2.5 billion in 1950 to 5.3 billion in 1990, a 100% increase. By 2050, the population will have doubled again. The pressure to provide higher quality, more abundant harvest on less acreage and with fewer farmers will continue to grow. It will take all of the technology possible to meet the challenge of feeding the world's population.

In the 1960s, the breeding successes of the Green Revolution provided a partial solution to feeding the world's burgeoning population. The development and distribution of semidwarf wheat varieties was a major step forward in that process. But those varieties did not spring forth fully developed on their own. Dr. Norman Borlaug and others worked with varieties and germplasm that had been collected and improved by a USDA researcher, Dr. Orville Vogel.

What factors have contributed to this marvelous success story? How have breeders been able to make such large improvements? There have been several reasons. One of them has been the stability of the budgets of the State Agricultural Experiment Stations and the Agricultural Research Service (ARS) of USDA. These institutions have had a mission to develop a continuous stream of new and better plant varieties and have been provided funds to make it happen.

Another reason has been the availability of germplasm that a breeder needs to make improvements. When developing a new variety, a breeder crosses the best existing varieties and makes selections from the resulting offspring. Or, to incorporate disease or insect resistance and other desirable characteristics, the breeder may go to the National Plant Germplasm System (NPGS) to seek out varieties with the known traits of interest. This germplasm is then incorporated into new varieties.

Without stability in funding and access to the best possible genetic resources, it is questionable whether such notable progress could have been made.

History is probably the best predictor of the future. If we are to continue progress, we need to have adequate budgets for research and we need to have access to germplasm. The lack of either one of these ingredients will surely spell disaster or, at the very least, a slowdown in productivity. We need to be very careful about doing things for short-term monetary gain that will have long-term negative results.

Let's briefly examine the background for utility patents in plants. This is not a new concept. The Plant Patent Act was passed in 1930, and in 1970 the Plant Variety Protection Act was created. We have lived with them all these years and have still made this great progress–because, notwithstanding, germplasm and free exchange was practiced by everyone.

How has the situation changed? It has changed because of profit motives. When a private company develops a new variety, it expects a return on its investment and has every right to make a profit on its work. Why is a new variety of plant any different from a new chemical? The only way a private company can recapture its investment cost is to have exclusive protection for its product.

The legal basis for that right was set in 1985 when the *Ex Parte Hibberd* (227 U.S.P.Q. 443) decision removed the last barriers to traditional patent protection for new varieties of the higher plants, including agriculturally important crops. In the *Hibberd* case, the Board of Appeals and Interferences of the Patent and Trademark Office recognized the right of a scientist to patent germplasm in which a major improvement has been made by using tissue culture to select for genetic resistance to an analog of the amino acid tryptophan. This method allowed Hibberd to develop a corn line with a high tryptophan content.

But because the Hibberd patent describes the increase in tryptophan content rather than the particular genes for which he selected, he has, in effect, patented all genes that allow for a higher tryptophan level gained through inheritance. This creates serious implications for continued progress in corn breeding, especially for this trait. Essentially then, we now have a situation in which no other breeder can use the high tryptophan variety as the parent of a new generation except by agreement with the patent holder. And if the patent holder has a monopoly on high tryptophan corn, why would the patent holder want to allow another breeder to put that trait into a variety that would ultimately compete with the patent holder's high tryptophan variety? It is the same reason that Monsanto would not allow or license another company to use the formulation for glyphosate to develop a competing herbicide.

So the question is, will patenting of plants impede future genetic progress? Only after another decade or two passes will we be able to look back and make an objective evaluation of the consequences of patenting plants. We might, however, look into the past and ask "what if?"

Let us take rice for example. Rice breeding is another great success story. In the USA between 1950 and 1990, there has been a 149% increase in yield. Harvests went from 2242 pounds to 5590 pounds per acre.

An examination of 140 important rice accessions done recently indicates that their ancestry can all be traced to 22 introductions in the southern rice belt and 23 introductions in the western rice belt. What if the genes of several of these ancestral lines had been unavailable or financially out of reach of the breeders? If you eliminated parents that were themselves released varieties, would we have made such progress (Fig. 1–1)? And how expensive would the seed be if growers were paying a royalty for each ancestor?

Remember the semidwarf wheat varieties? What if Dr. Vogel had chosen, instead of widely distributing his first variety and its sister lines, to patent his material? Would there have been a Green Revolution in wheat?

The Agricultural Research Service has recently signed off on the release of a new corn germplasm that carries unique resistance to fall armyworm. What would be the consequences were the Agricultural Research Service to patent this release? Would this resistance only be available to the highest bidder? I don't believe that ARS, as a public agency, should operate in such a manner.

In addition to direct improvement in traits such as yield, a benefit of making germplasm freely available is that it increases the opportunity for genetic diversity. If we create a situation with patenting and royalties where breeders shy away from using all but a few publicly available varieties as parents, we are asking for the vulnerability problems that genetic uniformity can generate. For example, the Texas cytoplasmic male sterility gene was responsible for corn's susceptibility to the new strain of leaf blight and over 80% of the corn being grown in 1970 carried the gene. The southern corn leaf blight epidemic that occurred that year destroyed almost $1 billion worth of corn.

Plant breeders are continually searching for new genes responsible for yield, quality characteristics, drought resistance, insect and disease resistance, and other relevant raits. If we were to protect or patent the genes responsible for these traits we might end up creating a scenario in which the cost of royalties becomes a major, if not an overriding, factor in the choices plant breeders make as they select parents to create new varieties.

Let us briefly look at why the patenting act of 1790 was created—what was its purpose? Generally, the purpose was to reward inventors so they could make some money. It is recognized that unless inventors have some protection, there would be little incentive for them to develop new products. Even today, in some cases, commercial interests are reluctant to take up Government inventions unless they can do so with a patented product and with an exclusive license. Thus, in order to have some products used, it is necessary to provide patent protection.

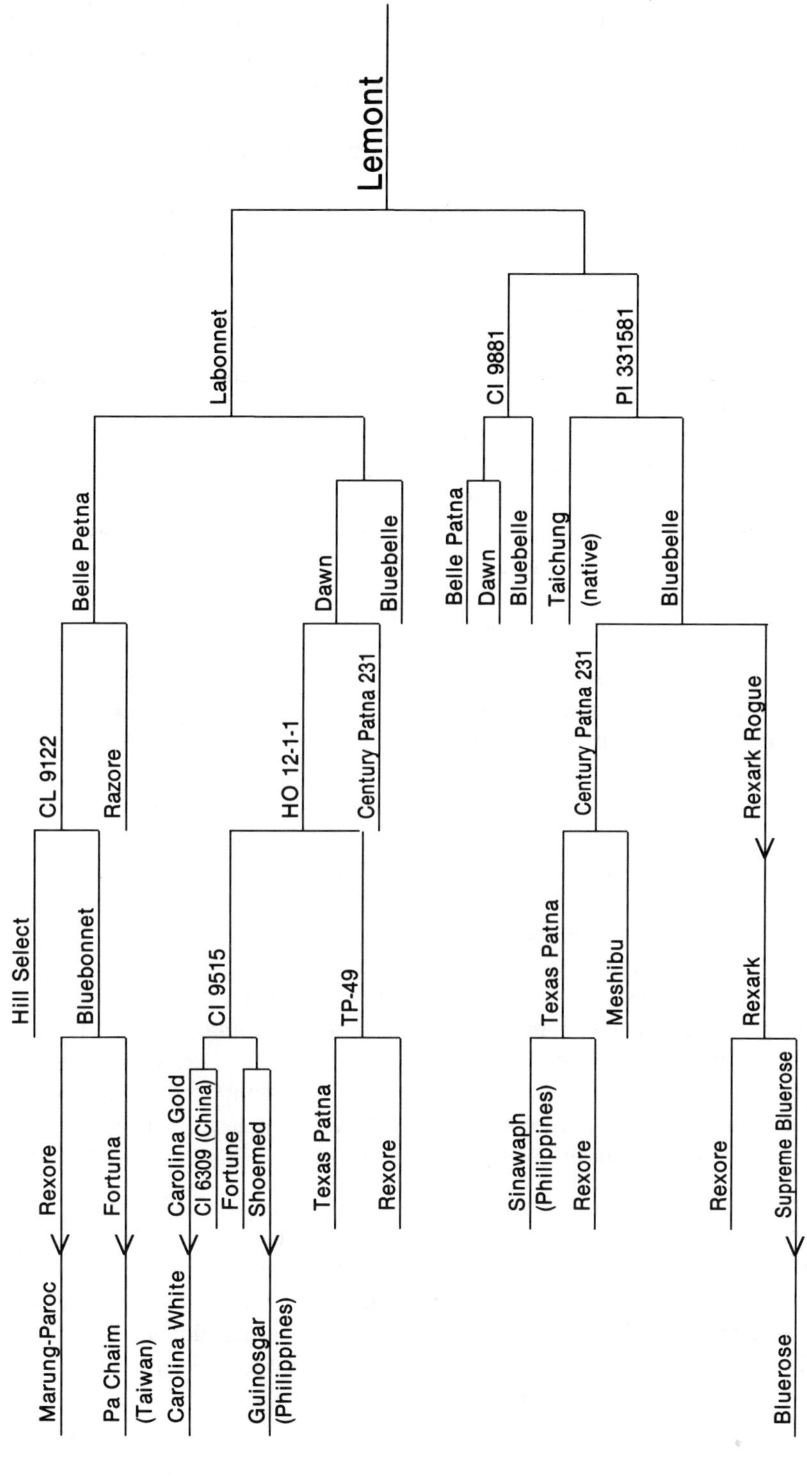

Fig. 1. Simplified pedigree of rice cultivar Lemont indicating the number of important ancestors used to develop variety.

Until recently, there has been little interest in patenting plants or germplasm by the public sector. Among the possible reasons might be a recognition among breeders that the great progress we have made in plant productivity is due in large part to the free exchange of germplasm. It might also be that protection is not needed for most plants in order to get new varieties used. On the contrary, farmers usually want to use a new variety before a researcher is ready to release it.

So why, then, is the plant breeding community so interested in plant patenting and protection? The only obvious reason is the expectation that such discovery and protection may result in an income-producing enterprise. Money seems to be the underlying force. To most of us, we have never seen a time when there has been so much economic stress in the public agricultural research system. Neither state nor federal funds are keeping up with inflation. Many budgets are actually being cut, and there is intense interest by all institutions to examine and exploit income-producing activities. In these times of tight budgets, the revenue from sales of new varieties might be an important supplement to barely adequate budgets at public institutions.

There are three important issues that need to be considered, debated, and brought to closure. These issues primarily concern the public sector because we cannot presume to tell private industry how to conduct its business. I identify these three issues as follow.

1. *Storage of patented germplasm.* There is general agreement both domestically and internationally that the collection, evaluation, preservation, and exchange of germplasm is a desirable activity. It provides for the long-term diversity of genes necessary to address continued enhancement of plants to improve yield, quality, disease, and insect resistance. Recognition of this fact was the basis for the establishment of the National Plant Germplasm System of which we are all justifiably proud. Its use is significant. Last year, we took in 8685 new accessions and honored requests for 285 762 samples of which 64 609 were sent to other countries.

We are currently re-examining our policy regarding the long-term storage of patented germplasm in the National Plant Germplasm System. Since the primary purpose of the National Seed Storage Laboratory is to preserve germplasm and have it available upon request from breeders, why should we go to the time, trouble, and expense to preserve something that is not available for use in new varieties? The argument that the germplasm will be available when the patent runs out in 17 years is not persuasive. This issue needs further study.

2. *Publicly funded varieties or germplasm.* In the public sector, research and testing that lead to the development of a new variety are mostly being paid for with public funds. Does that make the genes of a new variety developed in the public sector the property of the society whose tax dollars paid for the work? On the other hand, in order to induce industry to pick up a variety and

make it available commercially in today's market, it is often necessary for a public institution to be able to offer the seed or propagating material under an exclusive license. This requires the new variety be patented or otherwise protected by the Plant Variety Protection Act. There is little justification for spending public funds to develop new varieties or improving germplasm if they never reach the market place.

Does this mean then that plant protection is justified in some cases in order to ensure use and recovery of public investment but not in other cases when commercial use is guaranteed? In USDA, we have specific examples of each. For example, some nursery crops will not be taken, multiplied, and distributed for commerce unless they are patented and an exclusive license is granted to a supplier. On the other hand, new wheat or soybean varieties generally need no such protection for them to be used.

3. *Genetic progress versus making money.* This third issue is perhaps the most complex and serious question that we will face in the next decade. Stated quite simply, the question is "How can we continue to maximize genetic progress while at the same time realizing the economic benefits from patenting?". Although not proven, I truly believe that restricting the free use of germplasm by patenting will have a deleterious effect on future genetic progress. I am also pragmatic enough to believe that if we pit making money against genetic progress, making money will win every time. If that is true, then we need to find an accommodation or compromise between the two so that both goals can be realized.

For your consideration and discussion, I am going to suggest a solution to this dilemma. Let's have our cake and eat it too. Let's patent or protect plants and germplasm to extract economic benefits and at the same time allow free use for future breeding.

A compromise is possible between the conflicting needs of protecting intellectual property rights and enhancing progress in economically essential crops. It is possible to separate the issue of protecting return on investment for developing a new variety from the issue of the need for protecting the continued uninhibited improvement of our germplasm base.

The mechanism for this separation of issues is the use of a research exemption for varieties developed and patented by public and quasi-public research entities.

Such an exemption would allow the use of a patented variety as a parent in a breeding program without payment of royalties. The precedent already exists for a research exemption under the Plant Variety Protection Act. The right to use a protected variety in breeding programs without infringing on the rights of the original breeder is stated in Section 114. This type of research exemption could be expanded to include patented varieties.

It is not likely that granting such a privilege would create an economic hardship. Most of the profit from a new variety is made in the first 5 years. Even with the advent of genetic engineering, it would probably take more than

5 years to make crosses and complete field testing before a new variety is ready to market. Therefore, the possibility for direct economic conflict exists more in perception than in reality. Thus, a breeder would be able to immediately use protected germplasm for incorporation into future varieties and, at the same time, developers of the protected germplasm could reap the profits of sale. We recognize that the time allowed for realizing such profits would be shorter than at present, but this seems a small price to pay for keeping germplasm openly available for breeding.

The legal mechanics of a research exemption for germplasm or a patented variety can be worked out if the principals can reach a consensus on the concept of granting it. New legislation can be passed to create it if necessary.

Or the exemption could be created administratively. The 1990 Farm Bill language authorizing the Plant Genome Program could allow the Secretary of Agriculture to do this. According to the Farm Bill: "The Secretary shall require (when the Secretary considers it to be appropriate) licensing and patent agreements . . . on products and new uses, applications, technologies, or processes developed through the assistance provided under this section." All of the genes identified under the Plant Genome Program would fall under this provision.

The provision allows the Secretary to create agreements, at his discretion, to fulfill needs as he sees them. These agreements could certainly include a research exemption.

If we adopted such a policy, then the answers to the first two issues I raised would be obvious. There would be no need to question the appropriateness of putting patented germplasm in the National Plant Germplasm System. Likewise, the issue of protecting plants developed with the use of public money would be a non-issue.

The USDA has always been committed to the free exchange of germplasm. We do not want patenting to become a way to prevent people from improving on a variety because of economic or ideological reasons. A research exemption is an excellent way to ensure the vital, continued improvement of our crops.

I hope that all interested parties will seriously consider these suggestions as we seek to consolidate our thinking to develop policy on this most important issue.

5 Non-U.S. Protection Procedures and Practices—Implications for U.S. Innovators?

Barry Greengrass

International Union for the Protection of New Varieties of Plants
Geneva, Switzerland

Why does one need intellectual property protection of plant materials? Research into novel plant materials is long term and expensive. Plant materials frequently reproduce themselves after an initial release to the market place, depriving the innovator of an adequate opportunity to recover his research investment and/or to fund future research and development. Accordingly, among those interested in encouraging innovation in the field of plants, there has been interest in mechanisms, either legal or practical, or both, to protect the position of the innovator by providing him with a degree of exclusivity in relation to the production and sale of his innovation.

This paper addresses the implications of non-U.S. protection procedures and practices. As a basis for comparison it may be useful to remind readers initially of the forms of protection for plant materials that are currently available in the USA.

PROTECTION IN THE UNITED STATES OF AMERICA

Trade Secrets

The common law of contract and torts, laws relating to both moveable and immoveable property, and confidential and employment relationships, when combined with the physical nature of the plant material in question, have enabled plant breeders to maintain the exclusive use of certain genetic materials and information relating to such materials. This has resulted in certain varieties of plants, particularly F_1 hybrids, only being available from a particular supplier. The most obvious examples are F_1 hybrids, but forage and turfgrass varieties based on a limited number of parent clones, or the component lines of synthetics, provide other examples where the exclusive

 Intellectual Property Rights: Protection of Plant Materials, CSSA Special Publication no. 21.

possession of elite source materials by a breeder, together with information relating to their combination, ensures that only the breeder can offer authentic seed of a particular variety in the market place. If the variety in question is in demand, the breeder in question can expect to secure a premium price to fund his reseach investment.

If information and/or plant material is improperly acquired or misappropriated, the law will, in appropriate circumstances, provide a remedy for the plant breeder.

Protection of this kind led to the development of research based seed companies in the corn, sorghum, sunflower, sugar beet, vegetable, forage, and turfgrass sectors.

Plant Patents

To the USA belongs the distinction of being perhaps the first country[1] in the world to make specific provisions for the protection of new plant varieties. The provisions of the Plant Patent Act 1930 (now embodied in 35 U.S.C. sections 261 to 264) provide protection for asexually reproduced varieties other than those reproduced by tuber. A plant patent may be granted to any person who invents or discovers, and asexually reproduces a variety which has the following characteristics.

1. It is distinct (clearly distinguishable by one or more identifiable characteristics).
2. It is new (all the provisions of 35 U.S.C. section 102 are applicable in determining novelty).
3. It is not obvious (in theory the application of the normal nonobviousness criteria for the grant of a utility patent is called for; in practice, the application of this criteria to plants seems to call for the variety to differ from others by a characteristic that is totally different from the corresponding characteristic of similar existing varieties[1]. It is accordingly linked in practice to the distinctness requirement so as to require candidate varieties to be distinct by something more than a minor characteristic).

The plant variety must be described in the patent specification as completely as is reasonably possible. Only one claim is permitted which is specific to the plant variety shown and described in the specification. The grantee of a plant patent is entitled to exclude others from asexually reproducing the plant or selling or using the plant so reproduced.

The net effect of the plant patent system is the grant of a right, limited to the specific plant material, that constitutes a distinct and new plant variety. The protection granted is accordingly very similar to that granted under laws which conform with the 1978 Act (the 1978 Act) of the International Union for the Protection of New Varieties of Plants (the UPOV Convention) to which the USA is a party. By virtue of Article 37 of the 1978 Act, the USA is excused from full compliance with the 1978 Act in relation to plant patents and in fact first became a member State of UPOV on the basis of its Plant Patent Law.

The Plant Variety Protection Certificate

The Plant Variety Protection Act of 1970 (7 U.S.C. Section 2321) and provides protection for sexually reproduced plant varieties, with the exception of first generation hybrids, fungi, and bacteria, and thus partially fills a void left by the Plant Patent Act, which only protects asexually reproduced varieties. To secure protection, a variety must be novel, distinct, uniform, and stable. The owner of a plant variety protection certificate is entitled to prohibit others from selling or offering the variety for sale, importing or exporting the variety, sexually multiplying the variety for marketing, using it for producing another variety, and inducing others to perform any of the aforementioned acts. The scope of protection is limited to the variety.

There are two important exceptions from the breeder's right. First, any protected variety can be used to develop (as opposed to produce) a variety which is distinct from the protected variety. Second, farmers can save seed to plant the following year's crop. This is a provision found in many similar plant variety protection laws throughout the world. But quite unlike all other such laws in other countries, the U.S. law also permits a farmer whose primary farming occupation is not seed growing, to sell a quantity of seed to other such farmers without any obligation to the certificate owner.

Utility Patents

The 1980 decision of the Supreme Court in *Chakrabarty* v. *Diamond* [206 U.S.P.Q. 193 (1980)] established that, provided an invention involved a significant degree of human intervention, patents are available for inventions consisting of living material. As a result of this decision, utility patents are broadly granted in the USA in relation to products consisting of plant material as well as to inventions concerning processes relating to or uses of plant material. In a later case in 1985, *Ex Parte Hibberd* (227 U.S.P.Q. 443), the Patent Office Board of Appeals and Interference decided that, notwithstanding the existence of the special form of protection provided by the Plant Variety Protection Certificate for sexually reproduced plant varieties, utility patents could be granted for plant material including sexually reproduced plant varieties which fulfilled the criteria for the granting of a utility patent.

For the sake of readers who are not intellectual property specialists, I must mention that to be patentable an invention must be (i) new, (ii) industrially applicable, (iii) nonobvious, and (iv) the subject of an enabling disclosure.

Item (iv) requires that the invention be described so that a person skilled in the art to which the invention relates can reproduce it. In the case of inventions which consist of living material, it is frequently impossible, by following a written description, to reproduce precisely the same material. To overcome this problem, under U.S. patent practice, an applicant may deposit a sample of the relevant living material and the deposit supplements the description in the patent specification so that description and deposit together are deemed to constitute an enabling disclosure.

The granting of a utility patent entitles the patentee to exclude others from making, using, or selling the invention throughout the USA. The subject matter of the invention is contained in one or more claims distinctly claiming the subject matter which the inventor regards as his invention. The scope of protection afforded by a patent granted in respect to an invention concerning plant material can, for example, cover a broadly described category of plants or parts of plants, of plant material and, in the light of *Re. Hibberd*, one or more plant varieties.

The above represents the briefest of sketches concerning the availability of intellectual property rights for plant materials in the USA as a basis for comparison with other countries.

PROTECTION OUTSIDE THE USA

General

At the present time, the exercise by countries of their national sovereignty requires that each state be free to decide the forms of intellectual property protection that it wishes to exist within its frontiers, so that, in principle, one must look at each countries' national laws and practice in order to ascertain the precise position in each country. However, the need to strive for harmony in the provision of intellectual property protection has been recognized by countries for more than a century and most countries are party to one or more intellectual property treaties under which they voluntarily accept, in common with other signatory countries, common protection principles, practices, or minimum levels of protection. In any specific instance, however, it is necessary to examine the legal situation in each country separately in order to ascertain the availability of protection for any particular plant material, although international conventions, increasingly, simplify the task by promoting harmonization and reducing the scope for national differences.

I have emphasized that countries freely decide the levels and forms of intellectual property protection which they wish to provide. However, this may change if the current round of trade discussions taking place under the General Agreement on Tariffs and Trade (GATT) (the Uruguay Round) are concluded. Among the numerous topics covered by these discussions is one entitled

"Trade Related Aspects of Intellectual Property (TRIPS)." If the GATT discussions are consummated in an agreement which includes the outcome of the TRIPS discussions, countries which become party to that agreement will be bound to provide certain minimum levels of intellectual property protection and it seems highly likely that one of these minimum levels will require the protection of plant varieties either by patent or by a special system of protection for plant varieties or by a combination of the two[2]. However, the Uruguay Round has not yet been concluded, so that the decisions of countries concerning the provision of intellectual property protection for plant materials continue, for all present purposes, to be taken on a voluntary basis.

The following is a brief summary concerning some of the principle features of the provision of intellectual property protection for plant materials in countries other than the USA.

Trade Secrets

The law relating to trade secrets outside the USA also results from the complex interaction of laws, with considerable differences in approach among countries of a civil law or common law tradition. It suffices to say that in most countries, depending always, of course, on the inherent strength of their national legal institutions and administrations, breeders have been able to retain reasonable control of their exclusive genetic stocks. Accordingly the very same research based seed sectors as have developed in the USA with the aid of trade secrecy have similarly developed in many countries outside the USA.

Plant Patents and Plant Variety Protection

General. With the one exception of the Republic of Korea[3], the distinction between asexually reproduced plants for plant patents and sexually reproduced plants for plant variety protection (plant breeders' rights) does not exist today outside the USA. Countries that have chosen to offer a form of protection specially designed for plant varieties, protect plant varieties in one system irrespective of the mode of reproduction of the variety.

While various aspects of the technology used in the breeding of plant varieties may be protectable by patent or under laws protecting confidential information, many plant varieties are the result of breeding programs which address obvious objectives with known technology. Accordingly, many improved plant varieties fail to embody an inventive step (or to be nonobvious) so as to be eligible for protection by patent.

The fact that a plant variety does not embody an inventive step does not negate its economic usefulness to society. It is important to encourage the development of, for example, wheat varieties with, say, improved yield, disease resistance, and quality, although these are the obvious objectives of all wheat breeders.

Many of the most important features of crop plants, such as yield, are the result of the interplay of vast numbers of genes. Improvements in such features can only be achieved by the techniques of plant breeding involving selection within large populations. Conversely, the techniques of modern biotechnology are primarily directed to single, or very few genes, but offer opportunities to plant breeders that did not previously exist. Such technologies overcome the natural barriers between species enabling useful traits to be transferred between species (of both the plant and animal kingdom) and offer sophisticated means of increasing the precision of selection by plant breeders and of reducing the time required to develop new plant varieties. However, in the foreseeable future the new technologies seem unlikely to displace the existing selection procedures of plant breeders for many important economic traits.

The benefits to be derived from the existing selection procedures of plant breeders and from the new biotechnologies are cumulative. The one cannot replace the other. It is desirable that systems of incentives exist for both the new biotechnologies and for the results of plant breeding. Systems of protection specially designed for plant varieties must be created or maintained which are complementary to patent protection for biotechnological inventions.

In April 1993, there were 31 countries in the world (Table 1–1) which protected plant varieties in a special system and three other countries, Mexico[4], Romania[5], and the Republic of Korea, which protected plant varieties in hybrid systems with features of both the utility patent system and the special system. Of the 31 countries offering plant variety protection in a special system, some 23 were members of UPOV and had adhered to the UPOV Convention. The remaining seven countries had laws which conformed or were substantially modelled on the UPOV Convention and were widely expected to adhere to the UPOV Convention in due course. The UPOV Convention is in effect an agreement between countries to grant a minimum level of protection for plant varieties on the basis of standard criteria.

A significant number of countries which do not at present have special forms of protection for new plant varieties have proposals currently under discussion.

The 1978 Act of the UPOV Convention. Under the laws of all UPOV member States, and of the other eight countries mentioned, which provide special protection for varieties, a minimum scope of protection is granted on the basis of the criteria specified in the UPOV Convention[6]. Since the USA has adhered to the UPOV Convention, the general principles for the grants of protection under the U.S. Plant Variety Protection Act correspond in most respects with those of the UPOV Convention. Accordingly, the criteria which must be employed by UPOV member states[7] when granting protection are novelty (in the special sense that the variety must not have been previously commercialized), distinctness from other known varieties, uniformity, and

Table 1. Member states of the International Union for Protection of New Varieties of Plants (UPOV) and non-member states which protect plant varieties by other systems, April 1993.

	Non-member states		
Member states	Laws in accordance with UPOV	Laws substantively in accordance with UPOV	Hybrid system of laws
Australia	Argentina	Chile	Mexico
Belgium	Austria	Kenya	Republic of Korea
Canada	Norway	Zimbabwe	Romania
Czech Republic	Portugal		
Denmark	Uruguay		
Finland			
France			
Germany			
Hungary			
Ireland			
Israel			
Italy			
Japan			
Netherlands			
New Zealand			
Poland			
Slovakia			
South Africa			
Spain			
Sweden			
Switzerland			
United Kingdom			
USA			

stability. The variety must also be given a name conforming with rules set out in the Convention and designed to be its generic designation[8].

The object of protection under the Convention is the protected plant variety[9], and the minimum scope of protection afforded by member states must entitle the holder of the right to forbid others, without his prior authorization, from producing the propagating material of the protected variety for purposes of commercial marketing, from offering such material for sale or marketing it, and from using the protected variety for the commercial production of another variety[10].

The fact that the minimum scope of protection need extend only to production of propagating material for purposes of commercial marketing means that member states are not bound to include in the scope of protection production of such material that is not for the purposes of commercial marketing, for example, farm-saved seed. However, member States are expressly left free to grant a more extensive right than the minimum specified in the Convention. If a member state so chooses, it can include within the scope of protection seed production on the farm for the purposes of resowing on the farm. A saved seed exemption is accordingly not *required* by the terms of the 1978 Act of the UPOV Convention to be included in national laws, although statements to the contrary are often made. France, for example, has no saved-seed exemption in its plant variety protection law[11].

No UPOV member state other than the USA permits farmers to sell propagating material of protected varieties without the authorization of the breeder. Insofar as this is possible under the U.S. Plant Variety Protection Act, the Act would seem in the view of many commentators to provide less than the minimum scope of protection required by the UPOV Convention and accorded to plant breeders by the laws of all other UPOV member States.

The scope of protection under the Convention is expressly restricted so as to ensure that any protected variety will be freely available for use as a source of initial variation in developing other varieties[12]. The minimum periods of protection are 18 years for vine and trees and 15 years for all other plants[13]. The Convention requires member states to grant a right of priority[14] based on the earlier filing date of foreign applications and to provide applicants who are nationals or residents of other UPOV member states with the same treatment as it provides for its own nationals[15].

The Convention does not require member states to protect all species of the plant kingdom, but requires them, on accession to the Convention, to provide protection only for a minimum number of species. The minimum number of species which a member state must protect increases over time. A member state must protect at least 24 species 8 years after accession to the UPOV Convention[16]. Most member states protect all species of economic importance in their territories and many member states now provide protection for varieties of the whole, or substantially the whole, plant kingdom, but occasional gaps in the availability of protection may occur in some member States.

The Convention also calls for each state to examine varieties which are candidates for protection in the light of the criteria for protection[17]. The early practice of UPOV member states called for the variety to be grown in official comparative trials to ascertain its distinctness, uniformity, and stability. While this remains the predominant practice in most member states for species in which large numbers of applications are received, the USA bases its examination system on data provided by the breeder. A growing number of other member states require that the breeder grow the trial on which the examination is based in accordance with an official procedure involving some degree of official supervision.

Article 2 of the Convention forbids member states which have granted protection by patent or by breeder's right for a particular species of plant to grant protection by the other form of protection for the same species. This is the so-called "ban on double protection." It is not, however, a total ban on patenting but simply a ban upon granting patents and breeders' rights for the same species. The early draftsmen of the UPOV Convention thought that problems would arise if protection for the same species was granted in different systems with different criteria[18] (and perhaps with different notions of what constituted a plant variety!).

Protection based on the UPOV Convention has worked well and the years have seen a steady increase in the number of UPOV member States, in the annual number of applications, and in the number of certificates of protection which are in force[19]. Significant increases in private sector investment have been experienced in most UPOV member states after the introduction of protection and, with the possible exception of the USA where the saved-seed exemption creates special problems, there have been few, if any, difficulties in enforcing protection.

The 1991 Act of the UPOV Convention. The experience of operating the Convention over some 30 years and the technical and scientific advances which have been experienced over the same period led to the convening of a Diplomatic Conference to revise the UPOV Convention in 1991. The new 1991 Act of the Convention[20] has not yet entered into force, but most member States are now working on the changes in their laws that are necessary before they can ratify the new Act.

The main changes are as follow.

1. *Protected Species.* The 1991 Act requires member states, after certain transitional periods, to protect varieties of all plant genera and species[21]. In the future, if a breeder commences a program with a totally new species, he will know that when he finally produces a variety in, say, 10 or 15 years' time, protection will be available. This was not always the case under the existing Convention.

2. *The Breeder's Right in Relation to the Production of Propagating Material.* Under the existing Convention, as already explained, the minimum right of the breeder in relation to the production of reproductive material extends only to production for the purposes of commercial marketing of the material. This has, what some may consider to be the advantage, that growers of crops, such as wheat and soybean, can save their own seed on a traditional basis without infringing the breeder's right but the disadvantage, for example, that a person planting an orchard or other plantation can buy one plant which he propagates to plant a whole orchard or plantation with no obligation to the breeder in respect of the propagated material. The potential for this kind of abuse has increased considerably with the advent of modern tissue culture. F_1 hybrid vegetable plants can now, for example, be propagated within a horticultural production unit without calling upon the breeder for further seed supplies and plant parts can be multiplied in an industrial fermenter. It seems clear that activities of this kind should require the breeder's authorization and are unrelated to the traditional saving of seed.

Accordingly, under Article 14(1) of the 1991 Act, the minimum scope of the breeder's right has been redefined so as to extend inter alia to all production of propagating material. Since this has the effect of eliminating the saved-seed exception and since some exemption of this kind seems to be a political necessity in many countries, Article 15(2) permits countries "within reasonable limits and subject to the safeguarding of the legitimate interests of the breeder'' to exclude farm-saved seed from the breeder's right. It is expected that most countries will give careful consideration to the application of this provision so as to limit the application of any exclusion to a few crops where the saving of seed has been an important feature.

3. *Extension of Breeder's Right to Harvested Material.* Under the existing Convention, the breeder's minimum protection normally extends only to the propagating material of the variety. This has the disadvantage that in the case, for example, of a variety bred to produce cut flowers, propagating material of the variety can be taken to a country where no protection is available and used there to produce an end product, in this case cut flowers, which are exported to countries where the variety is protected. The breeder can do nothing in many cases to prevent this practice.

Accordingly under Article 14(2) of the 1991 Act, the scope of the breeder's right is extended to the harvested material of the protected variety including entire plants and parts of plants if (i) they are obtained through the unauthorized use of propagating material of the protected variety, and (ii) unless the breeder has had reasonable opportunity to exercise his right in relation to the said propagating material.

The first condition is self-explanatory and the second results from the reluctance of some UPOV member States to leave the breeder free to choose whether he will exercise his rights in relation, for example in the case of wheat, to the seed or to the grain.

Article 14(3), which is facultative only, envisages a further extension of protection to the direct product of harvested material falling within Article 14(2) but subject to similar restrictive conditions to those set out in Article 14(2).

4. *Essential Derivation.* Under the 1978 Act, any variety is protectable which, inter alia, is clearly distinguishable, at the time of application, by one or more important characteristics from other commonly known varieties and any protected variety may be freely used as an initial source of variation for the purpose of creating other varieties (see Appendix 2, p. 159). These two features taken together create a situation in which an existing protected variety may be used as a source of initial variation and a variety selected therefrom may be freely exploited by the selector free of any obligation to the breeder of the protected variety, provided that the selection is clearly distinguishable by one or more important characteristics from the protected variety. Since the word ''important'' in this context has been construed to mean ''important for the purposes of making a distinction[22]'' and not ''important in the sense of having value,'' this has meant that a person selecting a mutant or a minor variant from an existing variety, or inserting an additional gene into it by back-crossing or some other procedure, can protect the resulting variety without rewarding the original breeder for his contribution to the final result. Typical examples are the selection of a color mutant from an ornamental

variety, the insertion of a single gene into a maize line by back-crossing (under the favorable conditions of the tropics, multiple back-crosses can be effected in 1 year), and more recently, the insertion of a single gene by genetic engineering.

The fact that the 1978 Act does not enable the breeder to prevent breeding approaches of this kind has been criticized as unjust by industrial circles and the 1991 Act seeks to remedy this situation by introducing the principle of "essential derivation." Article 14(5) of the 1991 Act provides that a variety which is essentially derived from a protected variety cannot be exploited without the authorization of the breeder of the protected variety. A variety is deemed to be essentially derived from another variety ("the initial variety") for this purpose when "(a) it is predominantly derived from the initial variety or from a variety that is itself predominantly derived from the initial variety while retaining the expression of the essential characteristics that result from the genotype or combination of genotypes of the initial variety; (b) it is clearly distinguishable from the initial variety; (c) except for the differences which result from the act of derivation, it conforms to the initial variety in the expression of the essential characteristics that result from the genotype or combination of genotypes of the initial variety."

Article 14(5) provides a non-exhaustive list of examples of acts that may result in essential derivation including the selection of a natural or induced mutant, or of a somoclonal variant, the selection of a variant individual from plants of an initial variety, back-crossing, or transformation by genetic engineering.

It is not envisaged that a determination concerning the essential derivation of a variety will be made by an examining office as part of the grant procedure, but rather that the question will be resolved between plant breeders by agreement or in the last resort through litigation.

The existence of the new principle should ensure in the future that those working as innovators in the field of plants will reach agreement before they undertake a program of activity which could result in varieties that are essentially derived from protected varieties. It is hoped that in the vast majority of cases amicable arrangements will be made between plant breeders and/or biotechnologists. If a plant breeder inserts a gene falling within the claims of an invention relating to genetic information (a "patented gene") into his variety, the resulting variety could fall within the scope of the patent enabling the patentee, in effect, to prohibit the exploitation of the variety. If, on the other hand, the patentee inserts the patented gene into the same variety, the breeder of the variety has no possibility at present to forbid the exploitation of the modified variety. In future, if a patentee of a gene inserts his patented gene into a protected variety, there will exist the possibility that the modified variety will be essentially derived and fall within the scope of protection of the protected variety. It is thought that the new balance established between the two systems in this way will facilitate the exchange of technology between plant breeders and biotechnologists.

Plant breeders and biotechnologists are described here as if they pursue fundamentally separate activities. UPOV is well aware that their activities may be pursued in one and the same organization or by one person, but it does still help, occasionally, for present purposes to talk of the two activities separately.

Some interesting discussion can be anticipated in UPOV circles in the months and years ahead concerning the practical application of this new principle[23]. It should be noted that there is no suggestion in the text of the essential derivation provision that the breeder of an essentially derived variety should be able to force the breeder of the initial variety to grant a license through some compulsory license procedure. This possibility was considered and rejected in the course of the revision process.

5. *Double Protection.* Unlike the first sentence of Article 2(1) of the 1978 Act, the 1991 Act is silent on the form of the breeder's right. It may take the form of a special sui generis breeder's right, or it may be called a "patent," or given any other designation provided it has the minimum substance provided for in the Convention. The 1991 Act equally contains no provision corresponding to the second sentence of Article 2(1) of the 1978 Act (the so-called "ban on double protection") so that a Contracting Party is, so far as the 1991 Act is concerned, free to protect varieties, in addition to the grant of a breeder's right, by the grant of other titles, particularly patents. A member State exercising this freedom to grant patents, in addition to the breeder's right, is free to decide whether an applicant must choose between a breeder's right and a patent, that is, if he applies for one, he cannot apply for the other, or whether he can apply for and be granted both the breeder's right and the patent. If, for any given variety, cumulative protection of this kind is obtained, the resolution of any conflict between the two kinds of protection is left to the legislation and courts of the member State where the titles were obtained and is not regulated by the Convention.

European Economic Community (EEC) Plant Variety Rights. In the EEC, consideration of the text of a Council Regulation (EEC) on Community Plant Variety Rights[24] has reached an advanced stage. This Regulation when adopted will provide for the granting of plant variety protection pursuant to a single application in all countries of the EEC. It seems likely to accord with the 1991 Act in all respects. Accordingly, protection will be granted for varieties of all species, protection will be extended to the harvested material of protected varieties (subject to the two conditions contained in Article 14(2) of the 1991 Act), the possibility will exist of a further extension of protection to the direct product of harvested material (subject to the two conditions contained in Article 14(3) of the 1991 Act), and provisions will be made to implement the essential derivation provisions of the 1991 Act.

The saved-seed exception is a difficult topic for the European legislators. I understand that in a very recent draft text such an exception is created which is limited to "agricultural crops" and which permits implementing rules to establish further reasonable limits to the exemption in the light of "the need to safeguard the legitimate interests of plant breeders." It will be interesting to see how this proposal fares as it comes under intense political scrutiny by agricultural circles in the EEC.

The Utility or Industrial Patent

Most countries in the world grant or recognize patents on the basis of criteria that are broadly similar to those used in the USA, that is to say, patents are granted for inventions that are novel, industrially applicable, non-obvious and which are the subject of an enabling disclosure. In the fine detail of the systems of many countries there are significant differences in both law and practice and particularly in the fields of technology for which patents are granted. Not only may there be doubt generally in some countries concerning the precise protection available for living material but in many cases plant varieties, as such, are expressly excluded from protection. In a count[25] in 1989, some 57 countries expressly excluded plant varieties from patent protection and in many cases these same countries did not offer a special form of plant variety protection so that breeders of new plant varieties were left totally unprotected.

In this paper, one cannot examine the precise situation in all countries which exclude plant varieties from patent protection. However, most countries in Western Europe exclude plant varieties from patent protection and since the European Patent Convention (EPC) also excludes plant varieties from patenting it is useful to adopt the European example as a basis for discussion.

Article 53(b) of the EPC (which is reproduced verbatim in the national laws of most European Patent Organization member States) reads as follows:

> "*Article 53: Exceptions to Patentability*
> European patents shall not be granted in respect of:
> (a) . . .
> (b) plant or animal varieties or essentially biological processes for the production of plants or animals; this provision does not apply to microbiological processes or the products thereof."

The current practice of the European Patent Office (EPO) under Article 53(b) of the EPC is based upon the decision in the *Propagating Material/CIBA-GEIGY* case (T 49/83, OJ EPO 1984, 112). The case came to the conclusion that the term "plant variety" when used in Article 53(b) had a meaning derived from Articles 2(2) and 6(1) of the 1961 Act of the UPOV Convention and accordingly meant a "multiplicity of plants which are largely the same in their characteristics and remain the same within specific tolerances after every propagation or propagation cycle," that is to say, it means a variety which is distinct, uniform, stable, and protectable under the UPOV Convention.

This *CIBA-GEIGY* decision seems somewhat simplistic to many plant variety protection specialists in its narrow understanding of what constitutes a variety, but its line of reasoning nonetheless leads to the conclusion that a plant or plants that are the subject of product claims in a patent are not necessarily "plant varieties" so as to fall within the exclusion of Article 53(b). Equally, if one goes up the taxonomic scale from plant variety, a group of plants (including perhaps a new species) described so as to embrace a multiplicity of plant varieties is not a "plant variety" and could in an appropriate case be the subject of a patent claim. Accordingly, under the present EPC practice a claim to a plant or a broadly defined group of plants does not fall within the exclusion and is admissible.

The *CIBA-GEIGY* decision is not without its critics and could yet be reviewed by court decisions in European Patent Organization member states. However, it is clearly an increasingly important foundation for the practice of the EPO in this field[11] and would probably also be followed in many national jurisdictions which include an exclusion identical to Article 53(b) in their patent laws.

This means that an innovator making an invention in the field of plants (say a source of virus resistance) and succeeding in incorporating that resistance in particular plants can, provided he satisfies the patent criteria, apply for a patent which claims the resistant plants. Provided that the innovator does not claim a plant variety or does not so describe his plants as to indicate that he seeks to protect specific plants (which are perhaps distinct, uniform, and stable so as to constitute a plant variety) then it seems likely that he will be granted a patent for his innovation.

Most discussion of this topic assumes that Article 53(b) applies solely to plants produced by the new biotechnology but there is nothing in Article 53(b) to support this conclusion. Breeding work involving the discovery of new sources of disease resistance, for example, would, provided it involves an inventive step, be similarly open to product protection by patent provided that the patent claims describe a class of plants in such a way that they cannot constitute a plant variety.

A frequent reaction to this situation is to pose the question "If one can have a patent relating to plants, the scope of protection of which can include plant varieties, what is the point of continuing to exclude plant varieties from patenting?" This is a fair question.

However, there is a counterpart to this question. A novel plant of a given species, in relation to which a patent application is filed, will only satisfy the criteria of the patent system if, inter alia, it embodies a feature which constitutes a nonobvious development when compared with a prior art. Typically, the existence of that feature in the plant will entitle a patent applicant to claim, on a generic basis, plants of the given species which embody the nonobvious feature. Such a claim will necessarily include within its scope all plant varieties which embody the nonobvious feature. Why then is it necessary to claim a specific plant variety, as such in the patent specification. This also seems a fair question!

In the aftermath of its Diplomatic Conference in 1991, UPOV is neutral in these somewhat theological arguments about whether plant varieties, as such, should or should not be the subject matter of patent claims. There is, however, one practical consequence of the granting of patents for plant varieties, as such, to which attention should be drawn. The UPOV system of plant variety protection is based on a variety's distinctness from other commonly known plant varieties, and also on its uniformity and stability. Where patents are granted for plant varieties as such, not only must the patent examiner give consideration to other known varieties for the purposes of novelty and the inventive step in the patent system, but each plant variety rights' office must give consideration to ''varieties'' which are the subject of patent applications and of granted patents (since these will frequently be varieties of common knowledge). A plant variety rights' office has no ready means of knowing whether the variety claimed in a patent application would or would not be regarded as a variety for the purpose of the plant variety protection system so as to be taken into account for the purpose of distinctness.

Difficulties of this kind will be largely academic if very few varieties, as such, are protected by patent. If, however, one can envisage a situation where many hundreds or thousands of varieties are protected in two separate systems with different criteria, severe difficulties may arise.

This kind of problem does not exist in Europe since patents are not granted for plant varieties, as such. In countries which do grant patents for plant varieties any future difficulties could be overcome if the breeder of a variety, which is the subject of a patent claim, were required to satisfy the patent examiner that the variety was distinct, uniform, and stable.

Where countries outside Europe have exclusions from patenting similar to Article 53(b) of the EPC, it seems possible that the interpretation of such provisions will in due course follow that adopted by the EPO. The position in countries which have exclusions based on different statutory language or upon jurisprudence is of course more difficult to define.

The main difficulty in securing patent protection for living material in Europe historically lay in the breeder or innovator's inability to so describe his invention as to enable another breeder, reasonably skilled in the art, to reproduce the same variety. As in the case of the USA, this difficulty is overcome in Europe by the system of deposit. This system, originally designed only for microorganisms, is gradually being adapted to other categories of living material, and while the deposit and maintenance of whole plants perhaps presents some difficulty, there is every reason to suppose that deposit will be generally available for plants in the future.

THE EXPERIMENTAL USE EXCEPTION

There was clearly particular interest in the Intellectual Property Rights Workshop (26-28 Jan. 1993, Washington, DC) in the subject of the availability of plant germplasm as an initial source of variation for selection purposes. The position under the 1978 and 1991 Acts of the UPOV Convention, where any protected variety may be freely used in breeding programs, has already been explained. The new essential derivation principle is not seen in UPOV circles as a modification of this rule. Any protected variety may still be freely used in a breeding program and, only in the event that the resulting variety is essentially derived, is there any restriction. Any competent breeder will know when he is taking a risk in this area.

The position under the U.S. patent law is quite different from that under the UPOV Convention. A patentee has the right to exclude others from making, using, or selling his patented invention. Apart from a statutory exception relating to the development and submission of information under federal regulation laws, any use of a patented plant during the patent term, including the use of a plant variety as a parent in a breeding program, will, in principle, constitute an infringement. There is, however, an experimental use exception established by judicial precedent. The exception exists where the accused infringer establishes that the use was either (i) for the purpose of ascertaining the verity, that is the truthfulness or exactness of the patent specification, or (ii) for the purposes of philosophical experimentation.

There must be doubt whether the use of a variety as a parent in a program aimed at developing further varieties, which would be protected and commercialized, would satisfy either of these criteria, even if the resulting varieties did not fall within the claims of the infringed patent.

In Europe, Article 31(b) of the Community Patent Convention[26] (which is not yet in force) contains an express experimental use exemption which has been incorporated into the national patent laws of a number of European countries. The Article provides that the effects of a Community patent shall not extend to "acts done for experimental purposes relating to the subject matter of the patented invention." The precise scope of this exception is not clear but many commentators assume that it would permit the use of a patented plant material as a source of initial variation. Of course, if the plant material (or plant variety) that results from the use of the patented material, falls within the claims of the patent relating to the patented material, then it would be an infringement of that patent to make use of or sell the resulting material or variety and in this respect the legal situation in Europe and the USA is the same.

SUMMARY

In the USA, protection is available by plant patent for all asexually reproduced plant varieties (in the every-day sense of the word "plant") with the exception of those reproduced by tuber, and by plant variety protection certificate for all sexually reproduced plants, with the exception of F_1 hybrids, fungi, and bacteria and by utility patent in relation to all plant inventions which fulfill the criteria of the patent system. Decisions concerning what form of protection to seek for a particular plant innovation involve consideration of the species in question, whether it is sexually or asexually reproduced, whether the plant material is "novel" for the purpose of any particular form of protection, and whether the innovation satisfies the criteria of the patent system (inventive step in particular). Other questions involve the expense or difficulty of securing one form of protection rather than another, the relative enforceability of each form of protection, and the scope of protection that is necessary to optimally exploit the innovation.

Outside the USA, protection is or will shortly be available in most developed countries by a special system of plant variety protection (but not necessarily in all countries for all plant species in the short term), and by patent for many plant related innovations, with the exception in many cases of plant varieties as such. The decision on the criteria to deploy in deciding upon the appropriate method of protection for plant material will necessarily be very similar to those used in the USA.

Does it matter that in Europe, for example, it is not possible to patent a plant variety, as such? I would suggest that insofar as it is possible in Europe to make valid claims in patents related to broadly described classes of plants (described by reference to a single or extremely small number of characteristics), the inability to secure a patent claiming a specific plant variety as such is relatively unimportant from the standpoint of the quality of protection available to innovators[27].

A major opportunity, available in the short term, to improve intellectual property protection for plant material in the USA and in other UPOV member states both in Europe and elsewhere lies in the implementation of the provisions of the 1991 Act of the UPOV Convention. The emergence of a system based upon the 1991 Act has some interesting implications for the future, particularly in view of the increased scope of protection which is now provided in Article 14 of the new text. If the United Kingdom, for example, decides to modify its national law and to ratify the 1991 Act, it should in due course become possible to protect a new banana variety in the United Kingdom, notwithstanding the fact that the variety will never be grown there, but with a view to taking action against imports derived from the unlicensed propagation of the variety in countries where plant variety protection is not available. Thus far, the United Kingdom, as an importing country, has probably been uninterested in the protection of bananas. The absence of any protection of the harvested material of a plant variety in importing countries has meant that it has also been a matter of no concern to exporting countries without breeders' rights if varieties were piratically exploited in their territories with no reward to the breeders of the varieties. This situation may well change in the future in relation to species where the harvested material of the variety moves in international trade.

In non-UPOV member states, the main effort lies in the promotion of a system in which plant variety protection and patent protection complement each other. If the jurisprudence of the EPO is widely adopted in relation to the exclusion of plant varieties from patenting, the existence or non-existence of such exclusions is largely immaterial. We can, I believe, look forward to a future in which the protection available for plant materials will progressively improve to the benefit of all.

FOOTNOTES

1. At the request of the editors, the expression "country" is used rather than state to avoid confusion with the states which comprise the United States of America. The expression "state" is retained when referring to member states of intergovernmental organizations.
2. See Article 30 of the Draft Agreement on Trade-Related Aspects of Intellectual Property Rights, Including Trade in Counterfeit Goods of 20 Dec. 1991.
3. See Article 31 of the Korean Patent Law No. 4207 of 13 Jan. 1990.
4. See Section 20 of the Mexican Law on the Promotion and Protection of Industrial Property of 25 June 1991.
5. See Article 11 of the Law Concerning Patents of Inventions of Romania (Law No. 64) of 11 Oct. 1991.
6. The International Convention for the Protection of New Varieties of Plants came into existence on 2 Dec. 1961. It has since been revised on 10 Nov. 1972, on 23 Oct. 1978, and on 19 Mar. 1991. All member States are bound by the Act of 23 Oct. 1978, with the exception of Belgium and Spain which are bound by the Act of 1961 as revised on 10 Nov. 1972. At 1 Apr. 1993, the Act of 19 Mar. 1991, was not yet in force.
7. See Article 6 of the 1978 Act (subsequent footnotes referring to Articles are references to Articles of the 1978 Act).
8. Articles 6(1)(e) and 13.
9. Article 1.
10. Article 5.
11. See the decision in "Revue du Droit de la Propriété Industrielle," 1987, no. 14, p. 81–91.
12. Article 5(3).
13. Article 8.
14. Article 12.
15. Article 3.
16. Article 4.
17. Article 7.
18. Actes des Conférences internationales pour la protection des obtentions végétales 1957–1961, at p. 51.
19. See "Plant Variety Protection Statistics," a report prepared annually by the UPOV Office for the Council of UPOV.

20. Available from the Office of UPOV, 34, chemin des Colombettes, CH-1211 Geneva 20, Switzerland.
21. Article 3 of the 1991 Act.
22. See in this context paragraph 7 of the Revised General Introduction to the Guidelines for the Conduct of Tests for Distinctness, Homogeneity and Stability of New Varieties of Plants, published by UPOV.
23. See UPOV document IOM/6/2 which was used as the basis for a hearing of non-governmental organizations in Geneva on 30 Oct. 1992.
24. See Proposal for a Council Regulation (EEC) on Community Plant Variety Rights, Notice No. 90/C244;01, published in the Official Journal of the European Communities on 28 Sept. 1990.
25. See Draft Memorandum prepared by the Office of UPOV in cooperation with the International Bureau of WIPO entitled "The Interface Between Patent Protection and Plant Breeders' Rights," at paragraph 47.
26. The Community Patent Convention provides for the grant of a patent by the European Patent Office which will have effect as a Community Patent in all countries of the EEC. It must be distinguished from the European Patent Convention under which the European Patent Office grants a European patent which takes effect in each of the member States of the European Patent Organisation as if it were a national patent granted by each member State. Some member States of the European Patent Organisation are not countries of the EEC.
27. See comments on this subject of Mr. Rudolf Teschemacher, Patent Law Director of the European Patent Office, reported in the Proceedings of the VIth International Symposium on the Protection of New Varieties, organized by CIOPORA in Munich, Germany, on 17 and 18 Sept. 1992.

6 Intellectual Property Rights in Plants

Nicholas J. Seay

Quarles & Brady
Madison, Wisconsin

In considering questions regarding the protection of invention in plants and plant varieties, one significant issue is the choice of form of protection. Unique among the products of modern biotechnology, in addition to the general utility patent system and the common law forms of protection, are the forms of U.S. and foreign intellectual property systems for protecting certain rights in plant varieties. This presentation will discuss, and contrast, the forms of intellectual property protection in plants.

A BRIEF INTRODUCTION TO THE FORMS OF INTELLECTUAL PROPERTY LAW PROTECTION FOR PLANTS

Intellectual property protection of plants has historically been considered different from other forms of technology. To better understand the purposes and objectives of the special statutory systems to protect inventions in plants, it is helpful to examine briefly the history of these special statutory systems. The special systems for plants are those created by the Plant Patent Act of 1930[1] and the Plant Variety Protection Act of 1970.[2] Other forms of intellectual property protection now available for plants will also be discussed, including utility patents.

Plant Patent Act of 1930

Before passage of the Plant Patent Act in 1930, it was the common perception that plants and other living organisms were not eligible for patent protection because living organisms were products of nature. This proposition was cited as the holding by the Commissioner of Patents in *Ex parte Latimer*[3] in 1899, which held that the fiber from the needle of an evergreen tree was an unpatentable product of nature. Another factor, at least as argued by the Commissioner in *Diamond* v. *Chakrabarty*, was that an ''obstacle to patent

 Intellectual Property Rights: Protection of Plant Materials, CSSA Special Publication no. 21.

protection for plants was the fact that plants were not thought amenable to the 'written description' requirement of the patent law.''[4]

In the drive to pass the Plant Patent Act in 1930, its advocates pointed to the contributions to society of plant breeders, notably Luther Burbank, and their great contributions to agriculture and horticulture. One rationale for the bill was to ''remove the existing discrimination between plant developers and industrial inventors.''[5] The Plant Patent Act of 1930 rectified these perceptions and addressed the concerns of breeders by statutorily recognizing that plant breeders created products that were more than mere products of nature. The Plant Patent Act specifically exempted plant patent applicants from the requirement of enabling written description contained in patent statute, Title 35 of the U.S. Code. The Plant Patent Act is now embodied in Sections 161-164 of Title 35.[6] Hereafter these sections will be referred to as the PPA.

The definition of patentable subject matter under the PPA is contained in Section 161 of Title 35 which provides:

> Whoever invents or discovers and asexually reproduces any distinct and new variety of plant, including cultivated sports, mutants, hybrids, and newly found seedlings, other than a tuber propagated plant or a plant found in an uncultivated state, may obtain a patent therefor, subject to the conditions and requirements of this title.
>
> The provisions of this title relating to patents for inventors shall apply to patents for plants, except as otherwise provided.[7]

The PPA thus extends patent protection not only to inventors but also ''discoverers'' of eligible subject matter. Note that protection is limited specifically to plants and plant varieties which have already reproduced asexually. This limitation was an inherent part of the PPA and was apparently premised on the perception that plants produced other than asexually could not be reproduced reliably true-to-type. The exclusion of tuber propagated plants, which includes only Irish potatoes and Jerusalem artichokes, was a political rather than scientific distinction. The rationale for this exclusion is that for tuber propagated plants the propagating and edible portions of the plant are the same.[8] The statute was subsequently amended to additionally exclude plants found in an uncultivated state.[9] By judicial interpretation the term ''plant'' as used in the PPA is defined in its lay, rather than scientific, meaning and thus bacteria are excluded from the Act.[10]

The PPA requires that a plant be ''distinct and new'' to be protected.[11] The term ''new'' has been interpreted not to mean that the plant did not exist previously, but to mean that the plant did not exist previously in a capacity in which it could reproduce itself.[12] The term ''distinct'' was intended to require that a variety covered by a plant patent must be distinguishable from any other previous variety of that plant.[13] The distinction may be established through any of a number of traits of the plant, including subtle biochemical distinctions rather than the usual morphological distinctions. The characteristics that a plant variety may have to make it "distinct" were listed in the legislative history of the PPA as follows:

> The characteristics that may distinguish a new variety would include, among others, those of habit; immunity from disease; or soil conditions; color of flower, leaf, fruit or stems; flavor, productivity, including everbearing qualities; perfume; form; and ease of asexual reproduction.[14]

The Senate Report also made it clear that the characteristics which distinguish the variety from others did not have to be superior, merely different.[15]

The provisions of Title 35 (Patents) that apply to utility patents also apply to plant patents granted under the PPA to the extent not otherwise provided.[16] Therefore, the provisions of Title 35 relating to novelty, utility, and non-obviousness are theoretically equally applicable to plant patents and utility patents, although courts have admitted difficulty in applying the requirement of nonobviousness to plants.[17] Nevertheless, it was held that a printed publication, which would bar a utility patent application, is not a bar to a plant patent, on the ground that a printed publication was nonenabling for a plant.[18] It has also been held that adding a new descriptive disclosure about the plant to the specification of a plant patent application is not adding new matter.[19]

The PPA contains, in Section 162, an exemption from the enablement compliance applicable to utility patents. However, this exemption is not absolute. Specifically the exemption is from noncompliance with the enabling written description requirement only "if the description is as complete as is reasonably possible."[20] It is now the policy of the Patent and Trademark Office, supported by judicial interpretation and federal regulations, that deposits of biological materials may be utilized to satisfy the enablement requirement for utility patent applications.[21] A question may arise if, and when, suitable depositories become available for asexually propagatable plant materials, as to whether or not deposit of such materials would then become "reasonably possible." At present, however, because no such depository exists, deposits are not routinely made or required for plant patent applicants, and the Patent and Trademark Office does not require such a deposit.

The grant of a plant patent gives the right to the patent owner to exclude others from "asexually reproducing the plant or selling or using the plant so reproduced."[22] A grant of a plant patent is, therefore, for a single asexually reproduced variety. Each plant patent application is permitted only one claim that is specifically to the plant shown and described.[23]

There is a split of authority as to whether a plant patent covers independent derivation of a plant having the same varietal characteristics or only covers plant material actually derived from the patentee's plant. The majority of reported decisions to date require that the patentee demonstrate such derivation to establish infringement, much in the manner of a copyright plaintiff.[24] One decision, in contrast, holds that the infringement inquiry should be directed toward the characteristics of the plant rather than its derivation.[25]

Another requirement for a plant patent application is that the applicant is required to designate a varietal name for the plant variety for which protection is sought. This requirement has been imposed in part to comply with the USA's accession to the UPOV Convention, Article 13 of which requires the examiner to examine varietal name.[26] Proposed regulations to detail the requirements with regard to varietal name designations covering both plant patents and utility patents which claim plant varieties have been twice issued for comment by the Patent and Trademark Office, but final rules have never been issued.[27]

As with the Plant Variety Protection System, discussed below, changes to the PPA may be necessary to bring it into compliance with the 1991 draft of the UPOV treaty.

Plant Variety Protection Act of 1970

In many ways, the Plant Variety Protection Act of 1970 (PVPA) is parallel to the PPA for protection of plant varieties that are sexually reproduced. Several factors were instrumental in the enactment of the PVPA. In 1961, the International Union for the Protection of New Varieties of Plants (UPOV) (discussed below) was instituted by a number of countries, to provide protection to seed plant varieties. The technology of plant breeding had developed sufficiently between 1930 and 1970 that there was a generalized perception that new sexually reproduced varieties could be replicated true-to-type in a way that was not thought possible in 1930. Sexually reproduced varieties are non-hybrid varieties or cultivars of plants that, for practical purposes, breed true-to-form when self-pollinated.

The document granted under the PVPA to protect the plant variety is a "Certificate of Plant Variety Protection."[28] The PVPA itself never refers to the protection afforded or its character as a "patent." In passing the PVPA, as Constitutional authority, Congress invoked both Clauses 3 (commerce clause) and 8 (patent clause) of Article 1, Section 8 of the Constitution.[29]

In many ways, the statutory scheme under the PVPA parallels the PPA with the principal difference being the nature of the plants protected, i.e., directed toward sexually reproduced rather than asexually reproduced plant varieties. As enacted in 1970, the PVPA excluded a number of named vegetables (referred to as the "soup vegetables"),[30] but this exclusion was removed by amendment in 1980.[31] Protection does not extend to fungi, bacteria, or first generation hybrid plants.[32]

The definition of protectible subject matter under the PVPA is a "novel variety" which is protectible if the variety possesses "distinctiveness," "uniformity," and "stability," with each term being defined.[33] Of these, "distinctiveness" is most critical and is defined to be a variety which "clearly differs by one or more identifiable morphological, physiological, or other characteristics."[34] As with plant patents, and in the absence of a judicial doctrine of equivalence, because the right afforded by the certificate is limited to the specific variety, a variety protected under one certificate cannot logically infringe the right granted under any other.

Procedurally, there are parallels to the utility patent system: a series of statutory bars,[35] requirements for the content of the application,[36] and a requirement for a seed deposit to be made with the Plant Variety Protection Office, a branch of the U.S. Department of Agriculture.[37] Infringement is defined to include selling the novel variety, importing the novel variety, sexually multiplying the novel variety, using the novel variety in producing (as distinguished from developing) a hybrid or different variety, using seed which has been prohibited from propagation, or distributing the protected variety to another without proper notice.[38]

There are several provisions of the PVPA which are not analogous to any provisions in the utility patent or plant patent systems: mandatory license,[39] a series of statutory exemptions for saved seed,[40] an exemption for sales by persons whose primary occupation is farming,[41] and a research exemption.[42] The farmer's exemption has led to the most litigation under the PVPA.[43] Recently, the Plant Variety Protection Office reported its first decision on a protest petition filed by a third party opposing issuance of a certificate of protection.[44]

What happens if one independently derives a protected variety, that is, re-creates the variety through a directed breeding program? The question of independent derivation as a potential defense to infringement is not specifically answered by the PVPA. The statute does, however, include a provision for an interference proceeding,[45] leading to the inference that independent derivation is contemplated. Moreover, the legislative history of the PVPA also recognized that independent invention, although infrequent, may occur: ''infringement is expected almost never to be by independent work, but by willful reproduction starting from the protected variety itself.''[46] In view of this language, independent derivation is unlikely to avoid infringement liability. However, an improved variety is presumably not dominated by a certificate on its parental variety.[47]

The 1991 UPOV revision, which the USA has signed, mandates several changes in U.S. law, but those changes have not yet been made. Legislation is being drafted to make those changes. The changes would be (i) to increase the term of protection to 20 years (and to 25 years for trees and vines), (ii) to extend the scope of protection to harvested plant parts, (iii) to limit the ''farmer exemption'' to prohibit ''over-the-fence'' sales and (iv) to expand the definition of infringement to include reproduction of the protected variety and sale of a variety derived from the protected variety if the variety expresses the ''essential characteristics'' of the protected variety.

Trade Secret

For some crops (i.e., corn) true-to-type seed is not generally sold to farmers, because of the yield advantage achieved through the use of F_1 hybrid seed. For a crop that is sold principally as hybrid seed, it therefore becomes possible to protect the inbred parent plant lines, which are necessary to make the hybrid, as trade secrets.

The practice of protecting inbred parent seed as trade secret has been used as a strategy by breeders of proprietary inbred lines. A previously unanswered question with regard to this strategy is the enforceability of the trade secret status of the inbred parental lines, since the parent plants must be planted outdoors and over a wide area. This contrasts to traditional trade secret case law which requires locked doors and security to establish trade secret status. However, this approach received judicial recognition in *Pioneer Hi-Bred International* v. *Holden Foundation Seed.*[48] In that decision, it was specifically held that the ''genetic message'' of a proprietary inbred line may be maintained as a trade secret and a right of action for trade secret theft may be pursued against an unlawful appropriator.[49]

A question left unanswered by the decision in *Pioneer* v. *Holden*, is the propriety of a strategy referred to as ''chasing the selfs.'' In a sufficiently large quantity of hybrid seed there will be an occasional seed that was self-pollinated by the maternal parent plant because of incomplete detasseling or incomplete male sterility. This self-pollinated plant represents the inbred variety of the maternal parent line. Such seed is freely, if unintentionally sold, mixed in with the hybrid, although the frequency is low. In *Pioneer* v. *Holden,* the defendant testified to the genealogy of its inbred line, an explanation for the derivation of the plant material which the court found to be contrary to scientific evidence and not credible.[50] It is unclear if the court could have reached the same decision had Holden adopted the ''chasing the selfs'' defense.

In any event, the enforceability of a trade secret right in a plant line offers an alternative form of protection to consider for those plant materials which are not sold as a product in that form.

Utility Patents

Prior to the Supreme Court decision in *Diamond* v. *Chakrabarty*,[51] which held living things could be patented, many patent practitioners, and most of the lay community associated with plants and the seed trade, believed that utility patents were not obtainable for plants. This may, in fact, have been the official policy at the U.S. Patent and Trademark Office. Nevertheless, utility patents were being granted for methods of treating and breeding plants. In fact, on a few occasions, the Patent and Trademark Office had issued utility patents which contained product claims to plants and seeds.

An early example, Boehm, U.S. Patent 2,048,056, describes a method of hybridizing plants that includes two product-by-process claims which begin "the plant which . . ."[52] Utility patents were granted on methods for making hybrid plants from certain crops and on methods for making new varieties.[53] At least two patents issued which claimed plants themselves.[54]

The reasoning of the Supreme Court decision in *Diamond* v. *Chakrabarty*, which established microorganisms as patentable subject matter, seemed, to most practitioners, just as applicable to inventions in plants. After the decision in *Chakrabarty,* the Patent and Trademark Office began examining patent applications on inventions in plants, and practitioners began to consider the availability of such protection upon encountering developments in plant technology.[55] Some Patent and Trademark Office Examiners also interpreted *Diamond* v. *Chakrabarty* to permit utility patents on plants.[56] The Patent and Trademark Office then began to resist issuing of utility applications on plants, perhaps feeling that the propriety of permitting such applications should be ruled on by an appropriate appellate body. An appeal promptly ensued, and in *Ex parte Hibberd* the Board of Appeals and Interferences held that claims to seeds, plants, and tissue cultures were proper subject matter for patentability.[57]

Hibberd contested the eligibility for patents of inventions claiming plant life. The Commissioner argued a variation on some of the arguments addressed by the Supreme Court in *Diamond* v. *Chakrabarty.* The Commissioner's position in *Diamond* v. *Chakrabarty* was that since Congress specifically passed the PPA in 1930 and the PVPA in 1970 to provide patent-like protection for these specific types of plant life, it must have been Congress' understanding that living organisms were not patentable subject matter.[58] In *Ex parte Hibberd* the Commissioner argued for a statutory construction asserting that because the patent statute, the PPA, and PVPA must be construed together, and under the rule of statutory construction specific statutes are found to control over a general statute, the PPA and the PVPA must be the exclusive forms of protection for plant life covered by those acts.[59] This argument was the basis of the Patent and Trademark Office's position, prior to *Hibberd,* that utility patents were permitted only for F_1 hybrids and tuber-propagated plants because those plants could not be covered under the PPA or the PVPA. The Board of Appeals and Interferences rejected this argument in *Hibberd* and found no conflict between the statutes.[60] The Board cited precedent that the availability of one form of statutory protection does not preclude or necessarily conflict with the availability of protection under another form.[61] The Patent and Trademark Office acquiesced to the holding of the Board, stating that claims to plant life are permitted.[62]

Forms of Protection Available Internationally

The PPA and PVPA are the U.S. statutes intended to be part of a system of international protection of rights to plant properties, often referred to as "breeder's rights." These statutes exist in international form through a convention forming the Union pour la Protection des Obtentions Vegetales (the UPOV). The UPOV organization administers an international convention similar to the Paris Convention for utility patents requiring member states to provide the same rights to plant breeders of other member states as it provides to its own nationals. Most of Western Europe, Israel, South Africa, Sweden, Hungary, Japan, New Zealand, Australia, Canada, and the USA have enacted breeder's rights laws and joined UPOV. Mexico has committed itself to join UPOV in the North American Free Trade Agreement (NAFTA) agreement.

Under the European Patent Convention,[63] a specific exemption to patentability is created for "plant or animal varieties or essentially biological processes for the production of plants or animals; this provision does not apply to microbiological processes or the products thereof."[64] There has been much discussion about the meaning of this exception; some had speculated that it forbids patent protection to naturally-bred plants while permitting it for genetically-engineered plants. Other respected commentators suggested that the prohibition is only to varieties per se, and is not a bar to patents or generic inventions in plants.[65] The latter view has prevailed, and the European Patent Office now regularly examines, and allows, utility patents on plants, at least for claims not directed to a plant variety.

Stirred in part by the effect of the *Hibberd* decision in the USA, and also by the possibility that the European Patent Convention could be construed to permit utility patents on plants, UPOV began convening committees to consider various revisions to the UPOV Convention. While the UPOV text, at U.S. insistence, permits dual forms of protection, i.e., both patent protection and breeder's rights protection, in those countries that already possessed patent protection prior to enacting the breeder's rights protection, there was and is significant opposition to the availability of utility patent protection for plants among the constituent community served by UPOV, particularly in Europe. The 1991 version of the UPOV Convention changes the rules, by requiring member states to change their national law so that some gene inserts in a protected plant variety do not avoid infringement.

The relationship between the patent law and the plant breeder's rights law is still a subject of active debate in Europe. The European Commissioners, in a report several years ago, recommended that utility patents on plants be retained but that compulsory licenses be offered to holders of dominated plant breeder's right documents. Recently (Fall 1992), the European Parliament gave its opinion on patent issues, and proposed several amendments to the patent law including a ban on animal patents and a provision to introduce a "farmer's privilege" into the patent law. At the same time, the proposal to commence operation of a single European office of plant variety protection is advancing, and it may still become operational in 1993. Once accomplished, such an office would permit the filing of a single plant variety right application to cover all community members.

PLANT CLAIMS WHICH CAN BE OBTAINED IN UTILITY PATENTS

In deciding which form of intellectual property protection is appropriate for a given invention in plant technology, it is necessary to evaluate the type and scope of protection needed, which system of protection best fits that need. For a plant patent or a certificate of protection under the PVPA, the protection afforded is straightforward. Protection extends to plants of the variety as described in the document. The Plant Patent, unless the statute is changed, covers the whole plant only, and the PVP Certificate, unless and until the statute is changed, covers the seeds for the plant variety. If the statutes are changed to reflect the 1991 UPOV draft, plant parts would also be protected and derived varieties which retain the "essential characteristics" of the protected variety would be covered. Generic protection to groups of varieties or traits generally is not available.

In contrast, in the utility patent system, claims of varying scope and differing emphasis can be obtained depending on the nature of the invention and the prior art. It is instructive to examine patents which have been issued as examples both of the inventions which are protectible and of the strategies used to claim them. The examples below are vaguely, though perhaps inaccurately, categorized here simply for the purpose of illustration.

Claims to Plants by Variety

It is possible to obtain utility patent protection restricted to a specific variety of plant, regardless of its sexual or asexual reproduction. Such a variety may be claimed simply by its designation. For example:

"An inbred corn line having the designation HBA1"[66]

"Novel soybean varieties CX174"[67]

"A new and distinct plant variety, Yensen 3a, of *Distichlis palmeri, . . .*"[68]

"Inbred corn seed designated PHN73 having ATCC Accession No. 75205."[69]

Such varietal protection is also available for F_1 hybrid plants in addition to inbred plant lines. Such hybrids may also be claimed simply by designation.

"Novel F_1 generation hybrid corn seed DK672."[70]

"F_1 generation hybrid corn plant DK524."[71]

Claims to Plants by Phenotype

It is also possible to claim varietal plant inventions by means of phenotypic or combined phenotypic and genotypic characteristics. Consider the following claims in conjunction:

"1. Hybrid seed corn designated 3790.

"2. A hybrid corn plant and its plant parts produced by the seed of Claim 1.

"4. A hybrid corn plant with the phenotypic characteristics of the hybrid plant of Claim 2."[72]

The last claim would arguably read on any hybrid corn plant, regardless of genetic heritage, which has the phenotype described in the specification of the patent. Another interpretation is that, because it is a dependent claim, it includes the genotypic limitations of Claim 1.

If an inventor develops strategies useful to develop a series of inbred lines having common phenotypic characteristics, it is possible to claim the plants more generically. For example:

"1. An inbred line of tetraploid corn wherein said inbred line has the characteristics of . . . (any of 12 named inbred lines)."[73]

To the extent that a more generic trait is identified or bred into plant lines by conventional plant breeding techniques, it is possible to claim the trait either phenotypically or genotypically. Thus a trait which gives rise to a particular morphological plant trait can be claimed specifically by the phenotype of that trait. Consider the following claim:

"A recessive tall rice plant having elongated upper internode."[74]

Several patents have been obtained which disclose the derivation, either through tissue culture techniques or selective breeding, of resistance traits to specified herbicides. Often the claim is simply to a plant having resistance to the herbicide at a specified label. Consider the following examples of such phenotypic claims:

"32. A *Brassica napus* seed product consisting of a substantially homogenous assemblage of seeds which upon growth yield rape plants which exhibit a combination of cytoplasmic male sterility and cytoplasmic atrazine tolerance when applied as a foliar spray at a rate of 2 kilograms per hectare."[75]

"6. A maize plant wherein the growth and development of said plant is resistant to a herbicide sulfonamide at levels which normally inhibit the growth and development of said maize plant wherein said resistance is conferred by an altered acetohydroxyacid synthase resistant to inhibition by said herbicide at levels which normally inhibit the activity of an unaltered acetohydroxyacid synthase."[76]

Claims to Plants by Genotype

One can also claim genetic factors or genotypes in plants, whether created by traditional plant breeding, mutagenesis and selection, or by recombinant technology. Consider the following claim:

"8. A hybrid maize plant characterized by a genetic factor which confers an extra leaf phenotype, said genetic factor being capable of transmission to progeny substantially as a single dominant gene."[77]

Synthetic genes in plants can also be claimed at a plant cell level, thereby covering all plants which include a cell with the claimed gene. One patent claims all glyphosate-resistant plant cells which include a chimeric plant gene which encodes "a chloroplast transit peptide/5-enolpryuvylshikimate-3-phosphate synthase fusion polypeptide."

It is also possible to claim multiple different genetic factors as combined in the genome of the same plant.[78]

A specific plant and "radiation-induced mutants thereof,"[79] may be claimed, thereby arguably claiming a whole family of propagatable plants.

Possible claim subject matter is not limited to nuclear traits. Cytoplasmic traits may also be claimed: "A male-sterile corn plant comprising a cytoplasm conferring the property of male-sterility wherein said cytoplasm is LBM."[80]

Plant claims by genetic make-up can vary from the specific to the rather broad. A specific artificially-created mutant allele can be claimed: "Seed of *Brassica oleracea* comprising in its genome a homozygous allelic pair of dwarf (dwfl) genes from variety BBC-1 ATCC Accession No. 40376 conditioning for reduced internode length. . ."[81] This claim covers the specific gene created and any later plants of the species into which the allele is transferred.

Transgenic plant claim may cover specific genes, classes of genes, or even species of transgenic plants. The glyphosate-resistant cell claim above is an example of a claim to a fairly specific gene. Utility patent claims can be either specific or generic. Compare the following two claims:

> "A tomato plant cell comprising a DNA construct comprising a DNA sequence of at least 15 base pairs of a DNA sequence encoding tomato polygalacturonidase (PG) joined, in the opposite orientation for expression, 5′ to the 3′ terminus of a transcriptional initiation region function in plant cells."[82]

And:

> "A plant cell comprising a DNA construct comprising in the 5′–3′ direction of transcription a transcription initiation region function in a plant cell, a dsDNA sequence having as the transcribed strand a sequence complimentary to an RNA sequence indigenous to a plant cell, and a transcriptional termination region."[83]

Both of these claims are Calgene patents arising from the work which resulted in the Calgene "FlavrSavr" tomato. The first claim is limited to the tomato and the particular PG gene and the second claim is generic to all plants and all genes. Clearly the second claim dominates the first.

At least in one instant, utility patent claims can cover all transgenic plants of a given crop. Consider:

> "Cotton seed capable of germination into a cotton plant comprising in its genome a chimeric recombinant gene construction including a foreign gene and promoter and control sequences operable in cotton cells, the chimeric gene construction being effective in the cells of the cotton plant to express a cellular product coded by the foreign gene, the cellular product imbuing the plant with a detectible trait,

the cellular product selected from the group consisting of a foreign protein and a negative strand RNA.''[84]

This claim covers all transgenic cotton, regardless of how made, if the inserted gene construct expresses a protein or an antisense RNA.

This review of issued claims is not exhaustive. Methods of making or using plants are also patentable, and some products made by patentable processes can be covered. This review is intended to illustrate the variety of options and strategies adopted in obtaining utility patent protection for plant technologies. Any or all these and other strategies must be considered in the context of the invention created by a given applicant. The availability of claims of these various types is a factor to be considered in deciding which alternative form of intellectual property protection for plant technology is appropriate in a given instance.

PRACTICAL CONSIDERATIONS IN COMPARING ALTERNATIVE FORMS OF PROTECTION

A Plant Patent versus a Utility Patent

If a plant is asexually reproduced and its principal method of use in commerce will be by asexual reproduction, then the plant can be protected by a plant patent or by a utility patent. Each is discussed here. Because of the doctrine of double-patenting, there is some thought that these must be considered alternatives and that one must not do both.

It may seem from the above discussion of the flexibility inherent in the utility patent that it would usually be preferred, but this is not the case. First, it may be impossible to obtain utility patent protection for asexually reproduced plants of some types, simply because the enablement requirements cannot be met. For biological materials, it is possible to meet the enablement requirements by making a deposit of material in a recognized Budapest Treaty depository so that access to the biological material can be obtained by others after issuance of the patent. The Patent and Trademark Office (PTO) rules on the deposit of biological materials will require deposit of materials in either an International Depository Authority (IDA) established under the Budapest Treaty or other suitable depositories which are specifically recognized by the PTO.[85] Current practice for deposit of biological materials with an IDA is to deposit inherently stable and storable material, such as seeds or lypholized microorganisms. No IDA will presently accept living propagatable plant material (i.e., a cutting) that is incapable of cryogenic or other form of suspension. Therefore, there is presently no depository in which one could deposit many asexually reproducing plants. The proposed PTO rules further provide that other independent depositories may become recognized by the PT0.[86] Thus, at some time in the future, depositories may exist that accept such material, a so-called "arboretum deposit." Clearly, if a deposit is impossible, or impractical, the filing for a plant patent may be the only alternative.

Also, there may be a cost advantage, in most circumstances, to proceed by way of plant patent rather than a utility patent. Plant patents may involve less attorney preparation and filing time and may avoid deposit costs.

However, the limitations inherent in seeking protection under the PPA must be recognized. Parts of plants are not now protected, unless the statute is changed to match the new UPOV provisions. Therefore, if the plant product sold in commerce is a plant part, such as flower or fruit, filing a plant patent will not bar cultivation of the plant abroad or prevent importation of the plant parts, the flowers or fruit, in a way that a utility patent might. Furthermore, there may be no "doctrine of equivalents" for plant patents. The "doctrine of equivalents" permits a utility patent claim to be construed, in some circumstances, to cover articles which do not literally infringe the claim language. The sexual reproduction of patented plant material is not an infringement, nor is any biological material derived from sexual reproduction of the plant.

PVPA versus Utility Patent

Since the PVPA application also requires a seed deposit, the necessity for deposit does not create a distinction between the PVPA and a utility patent, although the deposit is a separate charge for utility patent and is included within the filing fee for an application under the PVPA. However, seeds deposited under the PVPA are not generally released to third parties and deposits for utility patents must be. One distinction between a certificate of protection and a utility patent is the scope of the protection. There is no provision for a doctrine of equivalents for a PVPA certificate. Thus, at least until the statute is changed to reflect the new UPOV provisions, any trait which distinguishes a potentially infringing plant from the variety norm as defined in the certificate of protection makes that plant outside the scope of protection afforded by the certificate. As plant genetic engineering becomes more routine, evasion of PVPA certificates will not be difficult.

Another consideration is that the PVPA has several statutory exemptions: the research exemption, the farmer exemption, and the provision for mandatory licensing, all of which have no counterpart in the utility patent laws. In particular, the farmer exemption has proven a difficult one for the proprietary right holder. There has been significant litigation against defendants who cultivated very large volumes of protected seed for sale to other farmers, but who sought to be considered a "farmer," for purposes of the exemption, to avoid the rights asserted by the holder of the certificate of protection.[87]

Again, on first impression, one may wonder what considerations could lead a plant breeder to choose the PVPA over the utility patent form of protection, particularly given the scope and flexibility of the protection available by a utility patent. However, there is a perception of cost effectiveness and reliability among plant breeders in the PVPA system that does not yet exist with regard to utility patents. Just as some industries are considered "patent conscious," and others are not, some proprietary plant breeders are accustomed to the PVPA system and its procedures and limitations, and may simply be reluctant to change as a matter of practice and procedure.

There may also be another reason to choose the PVPA. At present, many breeders consider that most new varieties are nonobvious under the utility patent law. Indeed, if claims to a variety are limited to an exact assemblage of traits, any particular assembly may be nonobvious. However, as breeding techniques and genetic mapping improve, this may not remain the case. Certain re-assembly of diverse traits may become very predictable, and therefore obvious. For protection under the PVPA, however, obviousness is not a test. Therefore, if one has a potentially obvious, but distinct, new variety, PVPA should be considered.

Trade Secret versus Utility Patent

Clearly trade secret is not an option in considering an inbred line of plant variety where true-to-type seed is to be sold to the general public. However, in the case of plants which are sold as hybrid seed, it is possible to consider trade secret protection for the inbred plant lines which are the parents of the hybrid seed as a viable alternative to patent protection. It is also worth considering phenotypic utility patent coverage obtained for the inbred parental plant varieties. An action based on trade secret must still demonstrate derivation, i.e., that the accused plant material is derived from the trade secret material. Proof of derivation of plant material is not required to establish a claim for infringement of a utility patent and so, presumably, phenotypic claims to plant varieties would be enforceable against any variety which meets the phenotypic characteristics, regardless of origin or method of creation.

For process inventions and plant technology, or for the creation of transgenic plants and similar developments in plant technology, the trade offs and considerations between trade secret and utility patent protection are not greatly different from considerations in other technical fields.

A POTENTIAL FUTURE ISSUE

Implied License and Post-Sale Restrictions

Suppose that a utility patent is obtained by a plant breeder on an inbred plant of variety X. The breeder of X then goes into commerce selling seed of the inbred variety X as a product of commerce to farmers. Unlike the PVPA, there is no farmer or other exemption for saved seed.

When a farmer buys the seed from the breeder, by law he receives an implied license to use the seed for its normal purpose. Presumably the normal purpose is growing plants from the seed under cultivation. However, if the plant breeds true to seed, the result of that cultivation, after the harvest, will be a greatly multiplied crop of the same seed. What is the farmer permitted to do with that seed? Clearly he must be able to sell this product as food or a commodity, since that is the purpose for which the farmer bought his seed, and presumably the breeder would have no quarrel with that. However, suppose the farmer sells the saved seed as seed. Presumably the breeder will have a significant quarrel with that. However, the method of determination of infringement of utility patents, as codified in Section 271 of Title 35 and the case law, does not envision a determination as to the intention of the accused infringer when he sells the product, i.e., whether he is selling it for seed or selling it for food. If the product seed may be sold as food, is a buyer who buys the seed from the farmer as food and then resells it as seed an infringer?

One way to solve this problem would be to impose a post-sale restriction on the use of the seed. Such a restriction might permit the product of the cultivation to be sold as a commodity, but forbid the purchaser from selling the seed saved from cultivation. Traditionally such post-sale restrictions on patented material are viewed with great suspicion, but at least one writer has argued that such restrictions may be permissible in certain circumstances.[88] Even if one seeks to impose such post-sale restrictions, there are practical difficulties in doing so. One court has recently held that post-sale restrictions as are commonly applied in commerce today to computer software are invalid both as adhesion contracts and due to federal preemption.[89] In a case not involving plants, a patent holder was permitted to require that the patented product he sold be limited to a single use.[90] If this restriction were used to limit the use of patented plant seed, it might effectively control post-sale use of the seed. Attempts to impose post-sale restrictions are likely to continue and need to be carefully considered if they are to be enforceable.

Similar questions may arise in a plant breeding program. Suppose a competitor of the plant breeder buys from the breeder seed of variety X but then crossbreeds it with variety Y in a program to make new variety Z. Is this an infringement of the plant on variety X? Presumably, if the second breeder grows up a stock of variety X for his own use, he is thereby "making," would come within the provisions of Section 271 and is an infringer. But suppose, instead, that the second breeder always buys his new seed stocks of variety X from the first breeder, thereby gaining an implied license to use the materials with each purchase. Since he never makes any new seeds of variety X, he should not infringe.

The extent of the activities which are or are not infringements of patents on living organisms, such as plants, will clearly take time to develop. The development of a body of license arrangements may make the respective rights of buyers and sellers more clear.

CONCLUSION

There are competing and alternative forms of intellectual property protection for plant materials. With regard to the utility patenting of plant materials, all the questions are not yet answered, and difficult issues remain for the future. Nevertheless, the alternative forms of protection available to the inventor who makes contributions to plant science have increased in recent years. The total fabric of these forms of protection offers significant help in protecting inventions in plants, to the profit of the inventor.

FOOTNOTES

1. Plant Patent Act, 35 U.S.C. §§ 161-164 (1982).
2. Plant Variety Protection Act, 7 U.S.C. §§ 2321-2582 (1982).
3. *Ex parte* Latimer, 1889 Comm'n Dec. 123 (1889).
4. Diamond V. Chakrabarty, 447 U.S. 303, 312, 206 U.S.P.Q. 193, 198 (1980).
5. S. Rep. No. 315, 71st Cong., 2d Sess. 1 (1930).
6. 35 U.S.C. §§ 161-64 (1982).
7. 35 U.S.C. § 161 (1982).
8. U.S. Patent and Trademark Office, Manual of Patent Examining Procedure § 1601 (5th ed. 1983 rev. 1988)
9. Act of Sept. 3, 1954, Pub. L. No. 83-775, 68 Stat. 1190.
10. *In re* Arzberger, 112 F.2d 834, 46 U.S.P.Q. 32 (C.C.P.A. 1940).
11. 35 U.S.C. § 161 (1982).
12. Yoder Bros., Inc. v. California-Florida Plant Corp., 537 F.2d 1347, 1378, 193 U.S.P.Q. 264, 291 n.34 (5th Cir. 1976).
13. S. Rep. No. 315, 71st Cong., 2d Sess. (1930).
14. *Ibid.*
15. *Ibid.*
16. 35 U.S.C. § 161 (1982).
17. 537 F.2d at 1378, 193 U.S.P.Q. at 292.
18. *In re* LeGrice, 301 F.2d 929, 944, 133 U.S.P.Q. 365, 378 (CCPA 1962).
19. Jessel v. Newland, 195 U.S.P.Q. 678, 685-686 (Comm. Pat. 1977).
20. 35 U.S.C. § 162 (1982).
21. 37 C.F.R. §1.801-809.
22. 35 U.S.C. § 163 (1982).
23. 35 U.S.C. § 162 (1982).
24. Cole Nursery Co. v. Youdath Perennial Gardens, Inc., 17 F. Supp. 159, 31 U.S.P.Q. 95 (N.D. Ohio 1936); *Yoder Bros.*, 537 F.2d at 1380, 193 U.S.P.Q. at 293.
25. Pan-American Plant Co. v. Matsui, 433 F. Supp. 693, 694, 198 U.S.P.Q. 462, 463, n.2 (N.D. Cal. 1977).
26. MPEP § 1612.
27. 52 Fed. Reg. 42,016 (1987) (advance notice of proposed rulemaking Sept. 9, 1987).

28. 7 U.S.C. § 2481 (1982).
29. 7 U.S.C. § 2581 (1982).
30. Pub. L. 91-577, Title III, § 144, Dec. 24, 1970, 84 Stat. 1559, *repealed* Pub. L. 96-574, § 20, Dec. 22, 1980, 94 Stat. 3352.
31. Pub. L. 96-574, § 20, Dec. 22, 1980, 94 Stat. 3352.
32. 7 U.S.C. § 2402 (1982).
33. *Ibid.*
34. *Ibid.*
35. *Ibid.*
36. 7 U.S.C. § 2422 (1982).
37. 7 U.S.C. §2422(3) (1982).
38. 7 U.S.C. § 2541 (1982).
39. 7 U.S.C. § 2404 (1982).
40. 77 U.S.C. § 2543 (1982).
41. *Ibid.*
42. 7 U.S.C. §2544 (1982).
43. *See, e.g.*, Delta and Pine Land Co. v. People's Gin Co., 694 F.2d 1021 (5th Cir. 1983); Asgrow Seed Co. v. Winterboer (Fed. Cir. Case 92-1048 decided Dec 21, 1992).
44. *In re* Argyle Bluegrass, 4 U.S.P.Q. 2d 1321 (U.S.D.A. Plant Variety Protection Office 1987).
45. 7 U.S.C. § 2504 (1982).
46. S. Rep. No. 1138, 91st Cong., 2d Sess. 11 (1970).
47. 7 U.S.C. § 2504(a)(1) (1982).
48. Pioneer Hi-Bred Int'l. Inc. v. Holden Foundation Seeds, Inc., No. 81-60-E, slip op. (S.D. Iowa, Oct. 29, 1987).
49. *Ibid.* at 72.
50. *Ibid.* at 65.
51. 447 U.S. 303, 206 U.S.P.Q. 193 (1980).
52. Boehm, U.S. Patent 2,048,056, Claims 5 and 6.
53. *See, e.g.*, U.S. Patent 3,710,511; U.S. Patent 3,842,538; U.S. Patent 3,832,801; U.S. Patent 3,903,645; U.S. Patent 4,102,079; and U.S. Patent 4,237,652.
54. U.S. Patent 3,861,079 and U.S. Patent 4,143,486.
55. Neagley, Jeffrey & Diepenbrock, *Section 101 Plant Patents—Panacea or Pitfall?*, 1 APLA Selected Legal Papers A-1 (1983 no. 2).
56. Bagwill, *The Legal Aspects of Plant Tissue Culture and Patents*, 21 Environ. and Appl. Bot., 383 (1981).
57. *Ex parte* Hibberd, 227 U.S.P.Q. 443 (P.T.O. Bd. App. & Inter. 1985). The language of 35 U.S.C. § 101 (1982) is as follows:

    > Whoever invents or discovers any new and useful process, machine, manufacture, or composition of matter, or any new and useful improvement thereof, may obtain a patent therefor, subject to the conditions and requirements of this title.

58. 447 U.S. at 310-11, 206 U.S.P.Q. at 198.
59. 227 U.S.P.Q. at 444.
60. *Ibid.*
61. 227 U.S.P.Q. at 446.
62. 1060 OG 4, Oct. 8, 1985.
63. Convention on the Grant of European Patents, *adopted* Oct. 5, 1973, 1977 Recueil des Traites et Accords (Fr.) 76, 1978 Gr. Brit. T.S. No. 20 (cmd. 7090) *entered into force* Oct. 7, 1977).
64. *Ibid.* at Article 53(b).
65. Crespi, *Biotechnology and Patents: Outstanding Issues* 8 EIPR 201 (1983).
66. U.S. Patent 4,594,810, Claim 1.

67. U.S. Patent 4,626,610, Claim 7.
68. U.S. Patent 4,762,964, Claim 1.
69. U.S. Patent 5,157,208, Claim 1.
70. U.S. Patent 4,607,453, Claim 2.
71. U.S. Patent 4,629,819, Claim 1.
72. U.S. Patent 4,731,499, Claims 1, 2 and 4.
73. U.S. Patent 4,705,910, Claim 1.
74. U.S. Patent 4,351,130, Claim 10.
75. U.S. Patent 4,517,763, Claim 32.
76. U.S. Patent 4,761,373, Claim 6.
77. U.S. Patent 4,713,532, Claim 8.
78. *See, e.g.*, U.S. Patent 4,654,465, Claim 18.
79. *See, e.g.*, U.S. Patent 4,616,009, Claim 17.
80. U.S. Patent 4,569,152, Claim 9.
81. U.S. Patent 5,107,064, Claim 1.
82. U.S. Patent 4,801,540, Claims 14 and 8 combined.
83. U.S. Patent 5,107,065, Claims 18 and 17 combined.
84. U.S. Patent 5,159,135, Claim 1.
85. 37 C.F.R. §1.803.
86. *Ibid.*
87. Asgrow Seed Co. v. Kunkle Seed Co., No. 86-3138-A (W.D. La.). Asgrow Seed Co. v. Winterboer (Fed. Cir. Case 92-1048 dec. Dec. 21. 1992).
88. Jeffers, *Restriction of Propagation of Patented Bacteria Sold by the Patentee—Can it be Done?*, 70 J. Pat. Off. Soc'y 137 (1988).
89. Vault Corp. v. Quaid Software Ltd., 847 F.2d 255, 7 U.S.P.Q. 2d 1280 (5th Cir. 1988).
90. Mallinckrodt Inc. v. Medipart, Inc., 24 USPQ 2d 1173 (Fed. Cir. 1992).

7 Update on Current Status of Patent Filings Involving Plants and Other Related Issues

Elizabeth C. Weimar

U.S. Patent and Trademark Office
Washington, DC.

PATENT PROTECTION FOR PLANTS

The statutory distinction between the two types of patent applications involving plants can be seen from the following.

Plant Utility Patents:

35 U.S.C. 101 lists the subject matter available for utility patents as ". . .any new and useful process, machine, manufacture, or composition of matter. . .".

Plant Patents:

The Plant Patent Act, in 35 U.S.C. 161, created a specific patent type for asexually reproduced plants, including plants found in a cultivated state, except for tuber-propagated plants.

The question as to whether a product made by the hand of man which is "alive," is patentable subject matter under 35 U.S.C. 101 of the general (utility) patent statute, was decided in the affirmative by the Supreme Court in 1980 (*Diamond* v. *Chakrabarty*, 447 U.S. 303, 206 U.S.P.Q. 443). As a result of this decision, the U.S. Patent and Trademark Office (PTO) has been patenting living material in the form of products or compositions with regularity, including plants and plant materials, such as plant cells in culture. The reasoning set forth in *Diamond* v. *Chakrabarty* was extended to the patentability of plants per se under 35 U.S.C. 101 of the general (utility) patent statute by the Board of Patent Appeals and Interferences of the Patent and Trademark Office in *Ex parte Hibberd*, 227 U.S.P.Q. 443, even though the same subject matter could be protected under the plant specific Plant Patent Act (PPA) of 1930 or Plant Variety Protection Act (PVPA) of 1970. This decision and the PTO policy which resulted are discussed in the Notice, "Plant Life-Patentable Subject Matter", 1060 Official Gazette 4, 8 Oct. 1985.

The Patent Examiner in the *Hibberd* application raised the issue that protection of plants under the general (utility) patent statute in addition to the variety protection offered by the PVPA and the PPA would create unnecessary confusion, as well as overlapping or contradictory protection. The Patent Examiner took the position that the two plant-specific acts excluded any other form of protection. However, the Board of Appeals found no legislative intent to restrict protection in the manner advanced by the Patent Examiner, after reviewing the legislative histories of the PVPA and the PPA. The Board held that the differences between the type of protection afforded by each of the two plant-specific Acts and by the general (utility) patent status would not present an irreconcilable conflict.

As noted in the *Hibberd* decision, the available protection under the utility patent statute differs from that of the PVPA and the PPA. Plant claims in a utility patent need not be limited to a single disclosed variety as is required by the other two Acts. Examples of some of the alternative claim structures used in plant utility patents include (i) plants altered via transformation, breeding, or mutation to exhibit an unexpected function or characteristic, (ii) plant parts, (iii) products which result from use of a specified process, (iv) seeds per se, and (v) plant cells.

The statutory distinction which affect the examination of plant patents versus plant utility patents involving plant subject matter include the following.

Description Requirements

The Plant Patent Act states in 35 U.S.C. 162 that "No plant patent shall be declared invalid for noncompliance with section 112 of this title if the description is as complete as is reasonably possible."

The first paragraph of 35 U.S.C. 112 of the general (utility) statute sets forth the description requirement for all utility patent applications, that "the specification shall contain a written description of the invention, and of the manner and process of making and using it, in such full, clear, concise, and exact terms as to enable any person skilled in the art to which it pertains, or with which it is most nearly connected, to make and use the same. . .."

The description requirement for applications filed under 35 U.S.C. 101 is more stringent than for Plant Patent applications, and requires that the explanation of the claimed variety should be presented in a manner which will distinguish that invention from other inventions and from plant varieties that are old and known to the artisan. An examination of a plant utility patent application will therefore include an analysis of the description provided in the application.

Enablement/Deposits

Examination of an application filed under 35 U.S.C. 101 of the general (utility) patent statute will include a determination as to whether or not the submitted description is adequate to enable one skilled in the art to make and use the claimed subject matter, as also required by 35 U.S.C. 112, first paragraph.

In some instances, a deposit of a biological material that is essential to reproduction of the claimed subject matter may be necessary to satisfy the requirements of written description and/or enablement for a complete disclosure of the claimed invention. The deposit rules are set forth in 37 C.F.R. 1.801-1.809. Although the specific details of the requirements for deposit are too extensive to relate here, these requirements basically provide assurance that biological material essential to the claimed invention will be available to the general public from a source independent from the patentee after the patent is granted. A deposit of biological material may be required where claims are specifically drawn to the plant product per se, or to any claimed invention for which reproduction of the claimed invention would require a specific biological material. For example, a claim to a fermentation method involving a specified bacterial strain or a claim to a hybrid plant might well require the deposit of biological material that is itself neither claimed nor separately patentable. The situation requiring parent inbred strains to be deposited to provide enablement of patentable hybrids may arise as a necessity in the instance in which the claimed hybrid cannot breed true.

Many questions have been raised concerning a requirement for deposit of parent inbred strains, particularly in the instance where the parents are themselves unpatentable, but the disclosure thereof is required to satisfy 35 U.S.C. 112 with regard to enabling the preparation of the hybrid. Of particular concern to an applicant making a deposit is the inability to control alternative uses of the parent varieties which have been made publicly available via deposit, such as in different breeding protocols, the products of which might not be covered by the claimed hybrid.

The requirement that the technology behind the claimed invention be reproducible and available to the public is the basic quid pro quo of the patent system. While the potential unintended, unprotected use of plant material deposited to meet 35 U.S.C. 112, is considered to be an undesirable result by those who would have protected that same material via trade secret, the importance of public possession of all of the technology behind the claimed invention is considered to outweigh the potential abuse.

The scenario of potential abuse is not limited to hybrid plant claims, but is common in other areas of technology related to biotechnological patent claims, such as fermentation methods which employ a specific bacterial strain to produce a specific antibiotic as well as claims drawn to microbial mutants. Also, from the general perspective, the requirement of a deposit of biological material is akin to the requirement for a complete disclosure, including how to make all of the ingredients that are essential to a patented composition, or, all of the starting materials that are essential to synthesize a patented chemical compound. In those cases where the essential ingredients or essential starting materials have previously been held as trade secrets, the same loss of control of the potential uses of those materials is involved in their disclosure for patent purposes of a derivative or composition containing them.

A deposit is not required in applications filled under the Plant Patent Act because of the less stringent disclosure requirements under 35 U.S.C. 162.

Sequence Rules

Another set of rules which are particularly relevant to applications filed in this area are the Requirements for Patent Applications Containing Nucleotide Sequence and/or Amino Acid Sequence Disclosure. The rules, 37 CFR 1.821 - 37 CFR 1.825, set forth the requirements and "how to" of presenting information in the form of a nucleic acid sequence or an amino acid sequence. For example, many of the applications directed to transformed plants present such information in describing the genetic material (nucleotide sequence) that is intended to be transferred to a plant host, as well as the protein (amino acid sequence) which it encodes. These rules require that applications with an effective filing date on or after 1 Oct. 1990 present the information in a computer reachable form (CRF), as well as list the information at the end of the disclosure in accordance with a specified format. This affords a more accurate examination involving searching those sequences and eliminates printing errors in published patents arising from separate, manual input of the sequence information.

Specific information about the sequence rules can be obtained from the following:

CRF Submissions: Meredith Beckhardt (STIC); telephone (703) 308-4212
Patent In Software: Art Powell (S&IR); telephone (703) 557-0400
Rules and Requirement: Group 1800; telephone (703) 308-1123

Terminology

A further distinction in examining applications filed under the PPA and plant utility patent applications involves the definiteness of terminology used in the specification and/or in the claims.

The general (utility) patent statute (35 U.S.C. 112, second paragraph) states that "(t)he specification shall conclude with one or more claims particularly pointing out and distinctly claiming the subject matter which the applicant regards as his invention".

This section requires that the language of the claims must make it clear what subject matter they encompass (see *In re Hammack*, 166 U.S.P.Q. 204,

208). This requirement is not only directed at the public being able to understand the scope of patent protection, but also to allow the examiner to properly compare the claimed subject matter to the prior art (see *In re Steele*, 134 U.S.P.Q. 292). Thus, an examination will include an analysis of whether the examiner can adequately determine what is being claimed, and in those instances in which the examiner concludes that the paucity of a particular description does not allow for the needed determination, then a rejection under 35 U.S.C. 112, second paragraph, will be made.

The PPA (35 U.S.C. 162) exempts a Plant Patent application from the necessity of strictly complying with the description requirement of section 112, so long as the description is as complete as is reasonably possible. The single claim in a Plant Patent application is a formal one which must be to the plant shown and described in the application. An examination on the merits with regard to what is known in the art is conducted in the examination of both a Plant Patent application and a plant utility patent application. Therefore, in both types of applications the adequacy of description must be analyzed in this regard.

Discovery of a New Plant Variety

A Plant Patent under 35 U.S.C. 161 can be obtained on a "discovered" variety as opposed to an intentionally developed variety, so long as the provisions of "growth in a cultivated area" and the capacity for "stable asexual reproduction" are met. Thus, sports are eligible for this type of protection.

In contrast, in plant utility patent application under 35 U.S.C. 101, mere discovery does not amount to patentable invention when the "hand of man" is not exhibited in the creation of the claimed product. Under the requirements, a "discovered variety" is considered to be a "product of nature" which is unpatentable under 35 U.S.C. 101. In the *Chakrabarty* decision, the Supreme Court gave the explicit example of discovering a plant in the wild as an unpatentable product of nature. Should the circumstance arise in a plant utility patent application that a claimed plant variety was discovered in a cultivated area, as opposed to being the result of a breeding or grow-out program, the mere fact that the discovery was in a cultivated area will not in and of itself remove the question of whether that claimed variety is an unpatentable "product of nature."

Double Patenting

While the decision in *Ex parte Hibberd*, concluded that the existence of the PPA did not preclude patenting the same variety under the general (utility) patent statute, it did not indicate that more than one patent term should run on the identical product. Thus, in those instances in which a claim in a plant utility patent application or patent is to the same variety claimed in a Plant Patent application or patent, a double patenting rejection will be made by the examiner. To the extent that the scope of the claim in the patents and/or applications is identical, two patents would not issue. However, if there is some difference in scope between the two sets of claims both patents may be issued provided that common ownership of the two will be maintained throughout the life of both patents and that the second patent to issue will expire on the same day as the first patent to issue. These requirements must be complied with in a document known as a Terminal Disclaimer.

CURRENT ISSUES RAISING LEGAL QUESTIONS

Availability of Plants

A recently published Board decision addressed the aspect of availability in *Ex parte Thomson*, 24 U.S.P.Q.2d 1618. The claims in this case were directed to a particular cotton variety and seeds of the variety. The issue was whether publications which disclosed the variety but did not specifically disclose how the variety was made, i.e., the specific breeding steps involved, precluded the patenting of the variety under 35 U.S.C. 102(b). This section of the statute bars the patenting of an invention which is described in a printed publication which was published more than one year prior to the date of the application for patent. An additional established fact in this case was that the variety was commercially available at least in Australia, more than one year prior to the application filing date. The Board agreed with the position taken by the Examiner that one of ordinary skill in the art would have had the necessary notice and the wherewithal to obtain the commercially available seeds and reproduce the claimed plant and seeds via conventional germination techniques, thus precluding the patenting of these materials. In distinguishing the facts of this case from those presented in *In re LeGrace*, 133 U.S.P.Q. 365, the Board considered the difference in the content of the publications at issue with regard to availability, as the rose plant advertised in the British plant catology in *LeGrace* could only be asexual reproduced if one had the plant, while the claimed cotton variety was sexually reproduced from the commercially available seeds.

Obviousness versus Distinctness

The requirement for a lack of obviousness in order for a claim to be patentable is established in 35 U.S.C. 103, and has been interpreted by case law to involve a determination based on three factual inquiries: (i) determining the scope and contents of the prior art; (ii) ascertaining the difference between the prior art and the claims at issue; and (iii) resolving the level of ordinary skill in the pertinent art. This approach is a general rule and applies to all patent application claims extending from a staple remover to sophisticated products involving computer electronics. The PTO does not develop separate criteria for each subject area. The decisions on patentability are made on a case-by-case basis applying the general test. Once developed, case law can indicate directions for the obviousness determination in a specific art area. However, as technology and skill of the artisan are dynamic, an absolute test for obviousness cannot be established for any specific art area and applied for an interminable period of time.

The UPOV concepts of ''distinctness'' and ''essentially derived varieties'' (see Appendix 2, p. 159) are used in determining patentability of the claimed variety over the known prior art variety for utility patent applications or PPA applications. Establishing that a claimed variety is different from a variety known in the art avoids the rejection that the claimed invention lacks novelty, as required by patent statute 35 U.S.C. 102 under either patent scenario. However, under either type of statutory protection the variety must also be non-obvious over known varieties in the art at the time the invention was made. The application of the standard of nonobviousness requires an assessment based on the knowledge of a person of ordinary skill in the plant art pertaining to the claimed variety. Thus, the assessment is not based solely on plant characteristics.

Grower's Contracts

In addition to barring a patent on an invention that has been described in a printed publication which was available to the public for more than 1 year prior to the application filing date, 35 U.S.C. 102(b) also precludes the granting of a patent on an invention which was in public use or on sale in this country for more than 1 year prior to the filing of the patent application. In those instances where the provisions of a grower's contract are brought to the attention of the Examiner and the contract allows for a ''conditional sale'' of the seed to the grower upon certain conditions such as ''unacceptable quality'' or a limit as to the amount of seed returnable to the assignee, the Examiner will raise the issue of an ''on sale bar'' under 35 U.S.C. 102(b). An Examiner might also find a prima facie case for a ''public use bar'' under 35 102(b) should the grower's contract not obligate the grower to secrecy concerning the material grown if the activity is more than 1 year prior to the application filing date.

EXAMINATION STATUS UPDATE

Filing Rates

The fiscal year 1992 (FY92) filings for Plant Patent applications filed under 35 U.S.C. 161 known to date are 337, which represents a decrease from the 454 applications filed in FY91. The projected filings for FY93 are about 370 applications. The FY92 filings for plant utility patent applications involving plant claims per se, filed under 35 U.S.C. 101, known to date are 214, which represents a slight increase from the 202 applications filed in FY91. The projected filings for FY93 are about 254 applications.

Application Pendency to First Action and Disposal

The present goal, which is intended to be attained by the end of this Fiscal Year, is to complete the first review and first communication to the patent applicant(s) of each application by 6 months from the filing date.

Staffing

In FY92, the number of examiners working full time on a plant-related docket increased from six to eleven. At the present time two experienced examiners work on a docket concentrated on Plant Patent applications, filed under 35 U.S.C. 161; four experienced examiners work on dockets concentrated on plant subject matter filed in utility application filed under 35 U.S.C. 101; and five relatively new examiners work on dockets which mix these types of applications. Nine of the eleven examiners have advanced degrees in plant-related subject areas, as well as research experience, which allows for an examination based on practical, technical expertise as well as patent experience.

Affirmance Rates at the Board of Patent Appeals and Interferences

In FY92, although there were a few Briefs and Examiner's Answers prepared in Plant Patent applications filed under 35 U.S.C. 161, no decisions were made in these cases by the Board. With regard to plant utility patent applications involving plant subject matter filed under 35 U.S.C. 101, the affirmance rate was approximately 72% in the decisions rendered by the Board in FY92.

Allowance Rates for FY92

For Plant Patent applications filed under 35 U.S.C. 161, approximately 350 applications were allowed, which represents a rate of approximately 84% of the applications in which prosecution was completed. For plant utility patent applications filed under 35 U.S.C. 101, 61 applications were allowed, which represents a rate of approximately 22% of the applications completed in that area.

8 Status of Intellectual Property Rights Protection From the Viewoint of the United States Plant Variety Protection Office

Alan A. Atchley

U. S. Plant Variety Protection Office
Washington, DC.

The USA provides protection for sexually reproduced varieties of plants through the Plant Variety Protection Act (PVPA) of 1970. Asexually reproduced varieties may be protected through the Plant Patent Act (PPA) of 1930. Finally, the basic patent law can be used through the granting of utility patents (UP) for methods of handling genetic material, and for traits and the genetic material that codes for these traits.

Each of these methods has peculiarities, and each has its enthusiasts and detractors. The U.S. Patent and Trademark Office (U.S. Department of Commerce/PTO) applies a standard of distinctness to asexually reproduced varieties under the PPA. It applies a novelty and usefulness standard to utility patents, and also requires that the invention be "nonobvious." The PVPA requires uniformity, stability, and distinctness (i.e., novelty) of any new variety. Novelty is established by demonstrating that the new variety is clearly different from all pre-existing varieties. Some of our concern as to the range of acceptable evidence of novelty lies in the lack of repeatability of some of the newer biotechnological assays of genetic constitution.

Some applicants seem to believe that PVPA protection is easier to enforce than other forms of protection; others seem to believe that UP protection is stronger and more extensive. Some appreciate that the PVPA does not require non-obviousness. Some state that UP protection is more expensive.

The following is a brief review of progress and prospects in plant variety protection.

TURNAROUND TIME IN THE PLANT VARIETY PROTECTION OFFICE (PVPO)

Recent staffing changes in the PVPO led to the buildup of a considerable backlog of applications. This backlog adversely affected turnaround time. More recent hiring, including the establishment of a new echelon of ''Associate Examiners,'' has made great inroads in that backlog for several important crops. It is the belief of the PVPO that not setting a time limit for examination of individual applications assures that the examination is more likely to be exhaustive.

A view of ''Plant Variety Protection in the 1990's'' was presented by a panel including the author at the 1992 Tomato Breeders' Roundtable in Sarasota, FL. There seemed to be a consensus that trade secrets are no longer a viable option for protection of plant varieties. There was concern at the number of early plant patents which had been overturned in the courts. The group was told that the way of protecting F_1 hybrids that has been used—that of protecting the parental lines—would not overwhelm the PVPO by sheer number of applications.

INTERNATIONAL OBLIGATIONS

The USA adheres to a multinational treaty named after the organization it established, the International Union for the Protection of New Varieties of Plants (UPOV). This treaty facilitates plant variety protection by nationals of the various member states in each other's countries. U.S. practice puts this country in an eccentric position within UPOV, and at least one of the changes thought necessary to bring U.S. practice into line with UPOV created political difficulties: The Farm Bureau opposed a ban on even incidental sales of treated seed. The tradeoff for any concessions is increased acceptance of U.S. varieties abroad. Breeders in some crops have no interest in exporting U.S. varieties. Others are keenly interested. Also, there could be increased availability of foreign varieties exported to this country; one of the major arguments in Canada in favor of their joining UPOV was that it would make available many improved varieties of potato in Canada.

Another matter involving intellectual property rights which concerns the PVPO is that of commercially obsolete varieties. The plant breeding community would like to exclude such from comparison with new varieties for which plant variety protection has been requested. The PVPA does not apparently allow such exclusion, even if the obsolete variety is actually biologically extinct. This has a negative impact on expeditious verification of novelty. The PVPO lacks authority to exclude obsolete varieties by regulation, so the PVPA will have to be changed. The exclusion of such varieties has the potential to entail extinguishing the breeders' rights of those who may have had some of the varieties protected.

FARMER EXEMPTION ("CROP EXEMPTION" IN THE PVPA)

The PVPA has a farmer exemption (FE) clause as well as an exemption for research. Some believe that the FE is too often abused and that it should be restricted in scope. It has been asserted that U.S. breeding in a certain market class of wheat for a large region of the country has come to a standstill because of such abuse. The most recent revision of the UPOV convention (March 1991) requires reducing the scope of the FE. Before the USA could ratify the 1991 convention, the PVPA would have to be changed. Various trade organizations have supported this move. The U.S. Department of Agriculture is now working with Congress in pursuing legislation to implement the 1991 convention.

NORTH AMERICAN FREE TRADE AGREEMENT (NAFTA) NEGOTIATIONS

This agreement is promising, in that Mexico has now agreed to join UPOV at some point. Both Canada and Mexico, however, envision exceptions to coverage of intellectual property. The consequences of these exceptions seem unforeseeable.

ESSENTIALLY DERIVED VARIETIES (EDV)

The preceeding issues are pending, but for each there is a clear sense of direction in which the PVPO would like to move. The situation with EDV is comparatively inchoate (see Appendix 2, p. 159). The following questions remain unresolved.

(i) What degree of similarity is a necessary and sufficient condition for a variety's being considered "essentially derived?"

(ii) Who determines whether a variety is "essentially derived?"

(iii) Is the measure for defining EDV to be different for different crops?

(iv) What role, if any, is the PVPO to have in defining "essentially derived," or in determining that individual varieties are "essentially derived?"

The position of the PVPO is that whatever decision is made on these matters should be a clear decision. If PVPO is not to decide what constitutes an EDV, then whoever makes such a decision should clearly state what criteria are to be applied. So far, it seems clear that a consensus has been reached, at least in UPOV, that EDV are protectable under the PVPA if they show a clear difference from each and every other variety and meet the other legal requirements.

In summary, the PVPO is following developments in intellectual property protection with great interest. We endorse the view of UPOV that patent protection and protection of breeder's rights, such as we provide, are properly viewed as complementary, rather than mutually antagonistic or competitive.

9 Science Based Identification Plant Genetic Material

R. Bruce Hunter

Ciba Seeds
Greensboro, NC

BACKGROUND

The USA is a member of the International Union for the Protection of New Varieties of Plants (UPOV). UPOV is an organization which serves as the international forum for countries interested in plant variety protection. Its primary objective is to provide a framework for the protection of the intellectual property of plant breeders. Protection should be designed to benefit the inventor or plant breeder as well as agriculture and society in general. There are currently 22 countries who have membership in UPOV. It is anticipated that the membership will continue to grow.

Any country can gain membership to UPOV as long as it amends its laws so that they will provide protection of new varieties of plants in a manner consistent with the UPOV Conventions. The USA joined UPOV in 1981. At that time, the U.S. Plant Variety Protection Act (PVPA) was developed to comply with the 1978 UPOV Convention. When a country becomes a signatory to a Convention, it is like signing a treaty agreeing to operate within the guidelines outlined in this treaty.

In March 1991, negotiations for a new UPOV Convention were completed. The U.S. Department of Commerce, through the Patent and Trademark Office and the U.S. Department of Agriculture (USDA), were responsible for negotiations on behalf of the USA. In order for the USA to become a signatory to this new Convention, the USA must amend the Plant Variety Protection Act (PVPA) to comply with the new Convention. This process is currently underway.

MINIMUM DIFFERENCE/ESSENTIALLY DERIVED

In order to have a workable approach to the protection of intellectual property, it is necessary to have some concept of how unique an invention should be to constitute as a new protectable entity. In this context, in the UPOV Conventions, certain sections provide guidelines to the degree of uniqueness required.

The PVPA of 1970, Chapter 4, Section 41 (A), states:

> The term "novel variety" may be represented by, without limitation, seeds, transplants, and plants and is satisfied if there is:
> 1. Distinctness
> 2. Uniformity
> 3. Stability

In section 41, "Distinctness" is the component of the PVPA that deals with the issue of "how distinct a new cultivar has to be from an existing cultivar to be eligible for protection and/or not infringe." The following is what is stated about Distinctness in the PVPA of 1970.

> Distinctness in the sense that the variety clearly differs by one or more identifiable, morphological, physiological or other characteristics (which may include those evidenced by processing or product characteristics, for example, milling and baking characteristics in the case of wheat) as to which a difference in genealogy may contribute evidence from all prior varieties of public knowledge at the date of determination within the provisions of Section 42.

The current PVPA thus qualifies a variety for protection if it varies in one or more characteristics from existing varieties. The weakness of utilizing this criteria for protection is that it permits the protection and marketing of new varieties which differ from existing protected varieties by only small differences of negligible economic value. These plagiarized varieties offer nothing extra to producers and result in one breeder profiting from another breeder's research without having contributed significantly to the invention.

In the March 1991 UPOV Convention, Article 7 discusses Distinctness as follows:

> The variety should be deemed to be distinct if it is clearly distinguishable from any other variety whose existence is a matter of common knowledge at the time of the filing of the application. In particular, the filing of an application for the granting of a breeder's right or for the entering of another variety in an official register of varieties, in any country, shall be deemed to render that other variety a matter of common knowledge from the date of the application, provided that the application leads to the granting of a breeder's right or to the entering of the said other variety in the official register of varieties, as the case may be.

In other words, the treatment of Distinctness in the most recent UPOV Convention is similar to that of the 1960 Convention and the current PVPA in the USA. However, the 1991 Convention contains an additional concept that also impacts on the question of Distinctness. This concept can be summarized under the term "Essentially Derived." The March 1991 UPOV Convention in discussing the "Scope of Breeders' Rights" (Chapter V, Article 14 (5) (a) (i) introduces "Essentially Derived" varieties (EDV) as:

> Varieties which are essentially derived from the protected variety, where the protected variety is not itself an ''Essentially Derived'' variety.

Section (5) (b) then goes on to state:

> For the purpose of sub-paragraph (a) (i), a variety shall be deemed to be ''Essentially Derived'' from another variety (''the Initial Variety'') when:
>
> (i) It is predominately derived from the Initial Variety or from a variety that is itself predominately derived from the Initial Variety, while retaining the expression of the essential characteristics that result from the genotype or combination of genotypes of the Initial Variety.
>
> (ii) It is clearly distinguishable from the Initial Variety.
>
> (iii) Except for the differences that result from the act of derivation, it conforms to the Initial Variety in the expression of the essential characteristics that result from the genotype or combination of genotypes of the Initial Variety.

It should be noted that 5 (b) specifically uses the term ''genotype'' as opposed to phenotype. It should also be noted that the convention has deliberately not defined in detail the concept of ''Essentially Derived'' in order to allow countries and organizations the opportunity to have considerable input into the interpretation and operation of this new concept.

The U.S. Seed Industry has broadly defined ''Essentially Derived'' as follows:

> A new variety should be considered to be ''Essentially Derived'' from a protected variety if, in view of its characteristics and method of development, it would be considered by a plant breeder of ordinary skill in the species to have incorporated in the new variety essentially the entire genotype of the protected variety. Factors to be considered in evaluating the method of development should include the source of the germplasm used and the breeding methods employed, including the reasonably expected results of these methods.

It further states:

> Varieties which are ''Essentially Derived'' but nonetheless clearly distinguishable from existing protected varieties qualify for legal protection but should only be commercialized with the consent of the owner of the original variety.

The concept of ''Essentially Derived'' is meant to (i) build a bridge between protection via patents and plant breeders' rights; (ii) decrease plagiarism in plant breeding; (iii) not restrict the breeders' exemption; (iv) be practical and not too complicated; and (v) exist in favor of and in relation to a protected variety.

The International Association of Plant Breeders for the Protection of Plant Varieties (ASSINSEL), an international organization of commercial plant breeders, have been a major force in promoting and providing input into the implementation of the new principle of ''Essentially Derived.'' ASSINSEL prepared a draft statement on ''Essentially Derived'' and in November 1991, the American Seed Trade Association (ASTA) Variety Identification Steering

Subcommittee decided that the ASSINSEL statement provided a good framework from which to examine how we will deal with the concept of "Essentially Derived." The Variety Identification Steering Committee was established by the ASTA to deal specifically with issues such as Minimum Distance and Essentially Derived. It is a subcommittee of the Intellectual Property Rights Committee of the ASTA. The Steering Committee has set up eight Crop Variety Identification Committees in order to be certain of obtaining input that represents both a broad spectrum of crops and a broad spectrum of viewpoints. ASTA also has representation on ASSINSEL as well as on the various ASSINSEL Crop Sections.

ASSINSEL has stated that an "Essentially Derived" variety (EDV) must meet the following criteria relative to the Initial Variety while retaining the expression of its essential characteristics: (i) clear distinction, (ii) predominate derivation, and (iii) genetic conformity. Note the term genetic rather than phenotypic conformity is used.

Following are several general aspects regarding the interpretation of Article (14) (5) of the 1991 UPOV Convention.

1. Dependency exists in favor of the protected variety.
2. The initial variety must be protected.
3. Dependency can only exist from one variety.
4. A dependent variety can be directly derived from an Initial Variety (IV) or from a variety that is itself predominately derived from an IV.
5. An EDV is based on genotype rather than phenotype (this is contrary to Distinctness).
6. The quantity of genotype taken over (conformity/genetic distance) is key.
7. Quantity of conformity can vary for different species.
8. Examples of methods of derivation that could lead to an EDV are (i) induced or natural mutant, (ii) somaclonal variant, (ii) selection of variant individuals from an IV, (iv) multiple back crossing, and (v) transformation.
9. Scientific and reliable means of determining genetic distance are required and might be Restriction Fragment Length Polymorphisms (RFLP), Random Amplified Polymorphic DNA (RAPD), Polymerase Chain Reaction (PCR), and Combining Ability.
10. Assessment should be made by species specific experts skilled in the art.
11. It is not intended that the Plant Variety Protection Office (PVPO) deal with the concept of "Essentially Derived." They continue to deal with distinctness, uniformity, and stability (DUS Test).
12. An EDV must be predominately derived from a given protected variety. If a variety has been developed without using that protected variety, there cannot be essential derivation.

13. "Essentially Derived" is the result of a process involving breeding method, objective, and breeding result and relates to the derived variety containing virtually the entire genotype of one of the varieties from which it was developed.
14. Dependency may or may not result from being "Essentially Derived." Dependency is a legal consequence of developing an EDV from a protected variety.
15. An EDV is an EDV forever. Even if the protection period of the IV has been exhausted, a variety derived from the first variety in a chain of EDVs remains and EDV and the remaining varieties in the chain will be regarded as EDVs from the IV. The new principle is meant to protect the initial breeder, not those making derivations.

On 5 June 1992, the ASSINSEL statement regarding the implementation of the new principle of "Essentially Derived" varieties in the UPOV Convention was accepted at the ASSINSEL annual meeting in Toronto, Canada. The ASTA had considerable input into this document.

IDENTIFICATION OF RELATEDNESS

When discussing the concept of "Essentially Derived," you will note that UPOV and ASSINSEL have emphasized genotype when referring to distance or similarity between varieties. In the past, the description of varieties has been based largely on phenotype. With the advent of such techniques as RFLPs, RAPDs, etc., it appears to be much more feasible and perhaps more accurate to describe a variety in terms of the genotype. In order to obtain the U.S. Seed Industry's perspective on the ability to determine genotypic distances, the Crop Variety Identification Committees of ASTA were asked the following question: Which reliable scientific methods of proof of genetic distance/conformity would be appropriate? The following are the answers provided, *to date*, by the various committees.

Corn. The committee agreed that the following would be appropriate for corn: (i) various biochemical and molecular assay techniques which may include isozymes, RAPDs, RFLPs, and antibody/antigen tests, (ii) breeding records and pedigree information; (iii) mid-parent heterosis measurements and combining abilities; and (iv) characteristics listed in Exhibit C of the PVPO Objective Description form.

The Corn Committee further states that no method in and of itself should be used alone in the determination of essential derivation.

Alfalfa. The committee agreed that the following tests or analyses were needed for alfalfa: (i) a joint and/or third party study of side-by-side tests for predetermined characteristics for which standard tests exist, and established public yield trials could be used to identify differences for yield and persistence; (ii) molecular marker analyses—isozyme, RFLP, RAPD, proteins, etc.—the difficulty being the uncertainty of current technology and related costs of differentiating adequately among varieties made up of a population of individual genotypes; and (iii) space plant observation trials with number of locations and replications established by the two parties—to include the two varieties and proper checks, agreed upon measured traits, material observed by experienced breeders at various stages during the growing season, and paired comparisons analyzed by appropriate statistics.

Cotton. The committee concluded that the methods described (RFLP, RAPD, etc.) would be appropriate as soon as the state of the art is such that reliable distinctions can be made in cotton. However, none of the members present were familiar enough with the status of the various technologies listed to judge their present effectiveness in cotton. It was felt that the final statement regarding scientific and reliable methods should probably be open-ended to include technologies that might evolve in the future for the purpose of determining genetic distance/conformity.

Sorghum. The committee agreed that the following would be appropriate for sorghum: (i) RFLP data, (ii) breeding history of variety development, and (iii) performance test and screenings from four locations, 2 years, and statistical significance at a level of 5%.

Soybeans. The most currently accepted scientific methods available which provide reliable information for proof of genetic distance.

Tomatoes. The committee agreed the following would be appropriate for tomato: (i) RFLP polymorphism, (ii) PCR techniques, including RAPDs to detect molecular polymorphism, (iii) electrophoretic analysis for isozyme variation, (iv) single gene mutants, and (v) quantitative traits over multiple locations.

Wheat. The committee agreed the following preliminary list would be appropriate for wheat: (i) testcross back to the IV to detect phenotypic and/or genotypic variation among the F_2 progeny; (ii) a review of the breeding records, pedigree information and, when appropriate, use of statistical evidence; (iii) grow the EDV and IV side-by-side and use the scientifically reliable methods to measure morphological traits; (iv) RFLPs, which are difficult in wheat at the present time; (v) RAPDs; (vi) PCR assayed by dot blot assays, radioimmunoassays (RIA); (vii) electrophoretic analyses of storage proteins and/or isozymes; and (viii) reversed-phase high performance liquid chromatography (HPLC).

The subcommittee recognizes that no single method is likely to be sufficient in determining whether a variety is essentially derived. However, a combination of several scientifically reliable methods should be used in each determination.

SUMMARY

The current UPOV Convention will serve to further strengthen the protection of intellectual property resulting from plant breeding by the addition of the concept of ''Essentially Derived'' (see Appendix 2, p. 159). The concept is meant to reduce plagiarism and, at the same time, assure germplasm access (breeders' exemption).

Both UPOV and ASSINSEL have stressed the role of genotype in helping to define relatedness (differences) between lines. Most ASTA Crop Committees attempting to examine the question of which reliable scientific methods of proof of genetic distance would be appropriate felt that several techniques such as RAPDs and RFLPs would be useful tools in helping to determine relatedness. However, other methods, including phenotype, could also contribute to determining relatedness. In addition, the genotype techniques are changing and improving very rapidly. Genotyping will become an even more powerful tool in the future.

10 National Legislative Issues

Terry L. Nipp

AESOP Enterprises, Ltd.
Washington, DC

Congress has just convened, with one of the largest turnovers in membership in some 60 years. A new President has just been sworn in, and the largest turnover in administration in 12 years is currently underway. In this environment, it is difficult to anticipate what will happen in the legislative arena. It is not just a matter of determining the issues of interest, but also a matter of determining what the priorities will be for dealing with issues. Many of the key Congressional staff who track biotechnology and intellectual property rights issues appear to believe that there are important issues that will be addressed, but they remain uncertain as to which issues and when. No clear leadership has emerged—yet.

Despite this uncertainty, it is possible to identify some of the concerns and events that may shape future debates regarding intellectual property rights. Public concern about the safety of developing and releasing new organisms will remain a critical issue. Regarding plants, this concern could be galvanized in response to the new rules proposed by USDA (November 1992) regarding easement of regulations on field trials of genetically engineered plants. The new rules may prove controversial enough to trigger Congressional hearings or legislation. Another issue that will drive debates about genetic resources will be the concern of key members of Congress regarding the use of federal funds for research on the development of herbicide resistant plants. It will be argued that such research may foster greater chemical and fertilizer use; moreover, some will argue that the benefits of such research will accrue to the private sector and therefore should be sponsored by the private sector. A bill to prohibit the use of federal funds for such research was introduced in the last Congress and will likely be reintroduced. Similarly, a bill was introduced in the last Congress that deals with labelling of genetically engineered foods; it is expected that it will be reintroduced and that it will receive significant public attention. More directly, a bill introduced by Senator DeConcini (D-AZ) during the last session (S.654), which deals specifically with the biotechnology patenting process, will likely be reintroduced.

The most critical question in anticipating future trends in the debates over biotechnology and intellectual property rights hinges on how important the issue will be to vice President Gore. In his book, *Earth in the Balance*, Gore spent a significant amount of time discussing the importance of biodiversity and the importance of protecting wild strains and centers of genetic diversity in developing countries. He supported some form of appropriate compensation to third world countries for the use of their genetic resources. At the United Nations Conference on Environment and Development (UNCED), he criticized the Bush administration for failing to sign the biodiversity treaty. Some in the USA expressed their fears that the language of the treaty was so broad that it might undercut patent protection rights negotiated in the General Agreement on Tariffs and Trade (GATT) and the World Intellectual Property Organization (WIPO). There was also a significant debate over the requirements for compensation to developing countries. Given Gore's personal interest in these issues, it is reasonable to assume that there will be reexamination of the U.S. position on the UNCED treaty. It is possible that this examination will result in a debate in Congress regarding the issues of just compensation and the protection of patent rights. In the course of these debates, there will be a search for ''workable models.'' It has been suggested that the arrangement developed between Merck & Co. and Costa Rica, where a fee was paid up front and royalties will be provided on marketable products, should serve as the model for legislated requirements.

11 Licensing Protected Property at Agricultural Experiment Stations

Eldon Ortman

Agricultural Research Programs
Purdue University

The primary rationale for a land grant university to be involved in germplasm development is to further science, to teach the science through classroom and practice, and to develop useful genetic systems and products. When useful discoveries evolve from programs, it is our fundamental philosophy that those discoveries should be made available in a useful mode as broadly and quickly as possible. The relatively recent opportunity to protect novel plant materials has added a new dimension to making discoveries available, i.e., patent and licensing. Also, it is our view that we should be good stewards of intellectual property just as with physical property, thus, we have taken a proactive position on patent and licensing.

In the Agriculture Research Programs at Purdue University we have protected and licensed discoveries in the plant sciences for well over a decade. The Office of Technology Transfer manages the patent and licensing process through consultation with the inventor, department, and school. In licensing we have several options: (i) make discoveries generally available with no license provisions, (ii) grant a non-exclusive license, or (iii) grant an exclusive license. Plant variety protection and patents have been used to protect plant material including corn, soybean, wheat, tomato, apple, and walnut. Licensing for these materials has included all of the above options.

As a land grant university, a fundamental question needs to be considered when licensing intellectual property: What option will result in the greatest general public benefit in the shortest time? The answer will vary greatly depending on the species of plant, the specific discovery, and the relevant private sector business scenario. The result of non-exclusive licensing is usually the creation of a more level playing field by general deployment of a discovery to a broad based clientele. An exclusive license is often appropriate when there is a very narrow or limited market, or the discovery needs further development before it can be successfully commercialized. The commercialization of a discovery may be stymied if a developer doesn't have an economic incentive. Also, an exclusive license may be offered to an agent who manages the intellectual property and guarantees to make it available through a sub-license to others on a non-exclusive basis. Another important matter in the goal of serving the greatest public good is to provide for a research exemption in a license agreement. This will greatly facilitate further advances and developments by removing the constraint for other researchers who might utilize an invention to create an improved product.

Establishing the value of a discovery for a license agreement is a complex matter involving assessment of the market in terms of the product's uniqueness, its relative competitiveness, and how long it will remain competitive. It is ultimately a matter of negotiation with the licensee. At Purdue we have several options in licensing, including an up-front research and development investment and various royalty payment schedules. University governance documents specify that the university will own all discoveries made by its employees and that royalties will be distributed equally to the inventor, the department(s) of the inventor(s), and the university. The university uses its portion of the royalties to pay patenting costs and has also established a fund where resources are available on a competitive basis to bring new discoveries to commercialization. There are no constraints on the inventor and department in the use of the royalty.

The process of licensing intellectual property at a land grant university is generally not a simple task. When considering the potential for licensing plant materials, the following represent some of the issues and questions which need to be considered.

1. Is there a clearly defined ownership position for the plant material as either intellectual or personal property? Is there other property that is critical or contributes to the successful use of the property?
2. What is the commercial status of the property, i.e., does it need further development or is it ready to be marketed and used?
3. Are there any existing agreements or understandings, written or verbal, involving the property?
4. Does the potential user industry have any familiarity with the property; for example, has the germplasm been grown and viewed in state, regional, or national nurseries?
5. What is the potential competitive position of the property? For example: (i) Does it embody a unique characteristic not found in similar plant material? (ii) Is the plant material best characterized as representing incremental improvement of general, existing characteristics of the plant material presently available? (iii) What is the potential effective commercial life expectancy of the property?
6. Are there existing standards or accepted norms for the species or commodity?

7. Are there existing public/private sector relationships pertinent to this or similar property?
8. What is the economics of the species? Is it the plant material which is the primary value or is it a downstream product of the plant material?
9. Are there points in the industry or the distribution system which can be readily accessed or utilized to manage or control the property?
10. What is the current system(s) for making similar property available, i.e., what is the nature of the industry for the species?
11. What is the amount of material available, how is it generated, how would it be made available for commercialization? What capability is required to bring the property to the marketplace? Does the inventor need to or want to have a role in supplying the property?

A review of the preceding questions would quickly lead to the conclusion that the licensing of plant material will be a species-by-species and trait-by-trait decision. The type of license to be pursued with plant material is not a generic decision but must be an individual decision tailored to the unique situation surrounding each property.

There are two fundamental approaches in licensing—exclusive and non-exclusive. The Agricultural Experiment Station would generally practice non-exclusive release of germplasm of primary agricultural species having basically incremental improvements in traditional characteristics. Germplasm of primary agricultural species would probably be ready to be marketed or require only minimal further development in order to be marketed. When the plant material to be licensed is a commodity with potential multiple business outlets in Indiana there is a high probability we will make the release through an agent. In Indiana that agent is generally the Ag Alumni Seed Improvement Association, an independent, not-for-profit corporation with a Board of Directors composed primarily of people from the seed industry. The release to Ag Alumni Seed is exclusive with the conditions that they increase the seed, advertise, exercise quality control, and market the material non-exclusively to the seed industry, but not directly to producers. There are mechanisms to assess a research fee on the commodity or apply the university royalty system. Both the fee and royalty are assessed across the seed industry in all states.

There are situations when an exclusive license arrangement is the logical approach, for example: (i) an exclusive license may be an essential element in negotiating research support for moving from discovery to commercialization potential, or (ii) there is a unique or limited market for the plant material. Where there is need for significant further development of a discovery before it can be commercialized, the offer of a first right of refusal to negotiate a license is frequently important in leveraging research and development funding. If it seems appropriate there are various constraints which might be placed on a license. One option we have exercised in an exclusive license is a limited time option, for example, 5 years at which time there may be a review or it may automatically become non-exclusive.

In summary, the fundamental objective for the Agricultural Experiment Station is to make available as broadly and quickly as possible the potential benefits of research discoveries. Frequently, licensing will facilitate that fundamental objective. The funds which might be derived from licensing should not be the basic reason for pursuing a license, as in a majority of situations, licensing of discoveries at Agricultural Experiment Stations will not generate significant funds.

12 Exemptions Under Patents and Certificates Covering Plants and Comments on Material Transfer Agreements

David J. Houser

Wisconsin Alumni Research Foundation
Madison, WI

STATUTORY FORMS OF PROTECTION FOR PLANTS AND PLANT MATERIALS

There are three types of statutory intellectual property protection available in the USA for plants: utility patents, plant patents, and Plant Variety Protection Act certificates. For each type of protection, limited exemptions exist under which the technology protected may be practiced for purposes of research or experimentation.

Utility Patents

Utility patents are the common, everyday sort of patent that you might get on a new mouse trap, drug, or manufacturing method.

Exemptions. The courts have evolved a research exemption doctrine for utility patents. They have sometimes held that utility patents are not infringed if the invention is practiced to verify that the invention will do what the patent says it will or to scientifically experiment on the technology involved for ''philosophical'' as opposed to profit-making reasons. Even under this doctrine, research usually is still an infringement if it uses the invention as a tool or means with which to do research on something else or if the research is a direct means of making a profit. Sometimes the supposed exemption is said really to be mere recognition of a de minimis use. If so, large scale activity might be found to infringe, even if it makes no profit and is pursued simply as philosophical research.

Plant Patents

Plant patents are a special type of protection specifically for new and distinct varieties of asexually reproduced plants, other than tuber-propagated plants and plants found in an uncultivated state.

Exemptions. One might expect courts to apply to plant patents a research exemption comparable to that applied to utility patents.

Plant Variety Protection Act Certifications

Patent-like protection issued by the Secretary of Agriculture for sexually reproduced, seed bearing plants, excluding fungi, bacteria, and first generation hybrids.

Exemptions. Certified seed may be used in ''research.'' However, the statute does not define the term, so the limits of use are uncertain. Furthermore, while it is an infringement to use protected seed to create a hybrid for commercial sale, one may use such seed legally to create an inbred line, which itself may be produced or used commercially. Inbred lines are self-fertilizing and breed true. Hybrids are made by cross fertilization and do not breed true. Inbred lines are certifiable and hybrids are not. Thus, a breeder does have the right to use a certified variety to make a new inbred line that itself may be certified or used commercially to make hybrids.

The statute allows farmers to sell surplus seed to other farmers so long as neither seller nor buyer are primarily engaged in producing seed for sale. Farm cooperatives or other third parties may not actively solicit buyers on a farmer's behalf. *Delta & Pine Land Co.* v. *Peoples Gin Co.*, 694 F.2d 1012 (5th Cir. 1983). Under *Asgrow Seed Co.* v. *Denny Winterboer*, (CAFC. 1992), a farmer qualifying under the farmer exemption is not limited in the amount of seed sold for reproductive purposes so long as (i) it is less than 50% of that farmer's disposition of that variety of seed, (ii) the receiver is a qualifying farmer, and (iii) the seller did not engage in growing up seed for ''marketing,'' i.e., extensive or coordinated selling activities, advertising, using intermediates or brokers, or similar extended merchandizing. The *Asgrow* court made a point of noting that the farmer's exemption relieves the farmer who sells seed of liability with respect only to some and not all of the actions labeled as infringing acts by the statute. The three requirements just listed must be satisfied.

Professor Donald Chisum (Chisum, *Patents.* §1.05[3]) reports that the North American Plant Breeders has successfully enforced the statute against growers who infringed by large-scale selling of surplus seed. However, he notes, none of these cases appear to have been appealed. The *Asgrow* v. *Winterboer* case is not inconsistent with this comment.

THE USE OF TRADE SECRETS AND CONTRACTS

The person who applies for a utility patent must make it possible for others to practice the invention in the best mode known to the inventor. Often this requires that a base pair sequence or samples of genes and the like must be made publicly available. Improvements made *subsequent* to filing the application usually need not be given out.

In contrast, inventors and breeders do not have to give the public access to plants covered by plant patents and Plant Variety Protection Act certificates. Those materials may be held as proprietary and treated as trade secrets, in effect.

Many companies are willing to distribute at least certain proprietary materials to researchers for non-commercial use, requiring the researcher to sign an agreement to get the materials. Such agreements are often called "material transfer agreements." For these arrangements to work, companies so releasing materials must be able to detect violations of the agreement and be willing either to invest in stopping such violations or to ignore them. Any company releasing materials to academic researchers needs to remember that, by their very nature, even well intentioned universities tend to communicate information and give out materials much more effectively than keep trade secrets.

Researchers receiving materials need to carefully weigh the possible down-stream effects of the agreements' terms and conditions, which can vary considerably from one company to the next. For example, the use of more than one borrowed material in research can lead to conflicting obligations to different companies.

The effects of material transfer agreements can reach far into the future, with unexpected and harmful results. For example, agreements exist that require the researcher to grant title or exclusive license rights back to the company under any invention made while using borrowed materials, and nonexclusive rights back under any invention made "as a result" of knowledge gained while using the materials. A researcher agreeing to terms like those may have to abandon related future research if it requires additional materials or financial support from a second company, with conflicting obligations to the second company. Having to abandon a major line of research in midstream can put a young professor's publication record and chances for tenure in jeopardy.

From a practical point of view, researchers—and especially academic researchers—should avoid borrowing materials that come subject to restrictions. At the very least, they should seek legal advice to make sure they understand exactly what they are getting into and where it may lead. Looking from the other direction, companies should avoid releasing proprietary materials, even under a material transfer agreement, when loss of actual control over the materials would be important to the company.

13 Exchanges of Protected Plant Material—Public Sector Perspective

Henry L. Shands

U.S. Department of Agriculture
Agricultural Research Service
Beltsville, MD

Historically, exchanges of germplasm between breeders and institutions, both nationally and internationally, have been generally open and free of cost. Public breeders have established personal connections with other breeders in their commodity networks and have exchanged considerable germplasm. Important germplasm exchanged in the past certainly includes the dwarfing genes which led to the Green Revolution.

The U.S. National Seed Storage Laboratory (NSSL) at Fort Collins, CO, at its beginning in 1958, solicited for seeds from breeders and institutions for germplasm storage security. Numerous public sector institutions and private seed companies have since contributed special collections when closing out programs or discontinuing interest in maintenance of special stocks after a scientist has left the program. In 1987, the National Plant Germplasm System (NPGS) initiated its current policy of making germplasm located in the NSSL base collection available to researchers through the repository maintaining the active collection. The NSSL is the designated base collection site of the NPGS, and its goal is to have a sample of all material within the NPGS. At any particular time, however, some items are not at NSSL since new materials must be increased to sufficient quantity at the responsible repository before they are entered into the NSSL.

Other genetic resources held in the optimal storage conditions of the NSSL include quarantined seed material awaiting processing at an approved site, "black box" security storage of genetic resources for other countries and international centers, and voucher specimens of protected varieties for the U.S. Plant Variety Protection Office (PVPO). Even after the NPGS has received a second sample of protected material, it normally refers requests to the owner of the material. The Plant Variety Protection Act (PVPA) is silent about

---

genebanks (and thus the genebanks' reproduction and/or distribution of certificated varieties); it is also silent on any requirement that the owner distribute the certificated variety. The law states, however, that the use and reproduction of a protected variety for plant breeding or other bona fide research shall not constitute an infringement of the protection.

As for the certificated material, the PVPO has issued certificates to private companies for inbred lines which those owners surely would not voluntarily distribute. Most companies will distribute their cultivars without difficulty, since, in reality, they are available for purchase in the open market. State agricultural experiment stations protecting varieties under the PVPA freely distribute their varieties to all requestors. However, there is an increasing uneasiness for some U.S. inventors about distribution to nations which do not protect intellectual property and some inventors have indicated an interest in having foreign licensees who will be accountable.

The USDA policy that all genetic resources held in the NPGS be available for research and use as parents in breeding programs troubles some institutions wanting to protect their property rights following deposition to the NSSL. They would like NSSL to preserve the genetic resources and simultaneously preserve property rights. That would require that the NPGS look at reasonable modifications to its current policy since such a change would result in a restriction to the use of the genetic resource. Questions regarding tracking and use of the material will surely cause problems in the case of foreign distributions. If the NPGS cannot continue to have an open distribution policy, will it be able to continue to argue for an open acquisition policy? The emotional attachment to the open and free exchange of plant genetic resources among many public sector institutions is strong and this opposition will have to be overcome.

U.S. and foreign scientists will have to contend with an increasingly diffuse U.S. system which will not be able to consolidate requests and provide genetic resources directly. U.S. researchers, public and private, may be unable to acquire protected foreign material through an NPGS unable to negotiate for third parties. International connotations become increasingly complex for protected genetic materials because of differences in national laws and policies.

The global germplasm system in the future may be evaluated by how quickly nations agree to establish an effective system to protect intellectual property. Transnational corporations may have an inherent advantage to move and broker material better than national genebanks (unless governments impose restrictions which in effect would be seizure of personal property). The United Nations Environment Programme's Convention on Biological Diversity (CBD) guarantees protection of intellectual property under existing international laws and offers not to restrict the availability of genetic resources. Exchanges of genetic resources will be governed by mutually agreed upon terms; at the same time, there will be a recognition of national sovereignty over those resources (as now reads amendment 3 to the non-binding Food and Agriculture

Organization's International Undertaking on Plant Genetic Resources). A pragmatic approach to dealing with complex international agricultural intellectual property issues is essential. The outcome is still in our hands and will be guided largely by our judgment.

In respect to its role in acquiring and distributing intellectual property material, the future of the NPGS is not clear. Should it become an accredited depository for patented material? It cannot do so with its current budget. Should it solicit and distribute patented material? The legal implications of tracking for the owner and/or brokering patented material availability and use may be difficult. What should be the NPGS policy for acquiring genetic resources from other countries? Should standards for patented intellectual property be different from non-patented genetic resources obtained from a country desiring to obtain the benefits from commercialization of its genetic resources? In the reverse flow to others, will the NPGS be accountable for material used by other countries and what legal instruments must it institute?

These questions will be answered by the directed evolution of USDA policy in respect to international treaties and laws of the CBD; General Agreement for Tariffs and Trade; World Intellectual Property Organization; the International Union for the Protection of New Varieties; international patent law; and U.S. laws on patents, plant variety protection, and technology transfer. Clearly, the USDA must do all it can to be sensitive to its role in improving crop productivity. Anything less than a workable policy enabling all scientists to continue uninterrupted in their breeding and research efforts will be unacceptable. This enablement does not stop with the USDA. It should be the objective for all nations and institutions concerned with food and agriculture, that is, every nation on the planet.

14 Exchange and Release of Biological Material: One Company's Perspective

Dennis R. Hoerner

Monsanto Company
St. Louis, MO

Researchers in the biological sciences have benefitted for many years by the receipt and exchange of biological materials. Releases of such materials were typically not covered by written agreements embracing restrictions on the use of such material, but rather by undocumented understandings between the parties, as well as ethical standards. Developments in the field of biological science since the latter 1970s, particularly genetic engineering techniques, have resulted in the ability to produce novel biological products (e.g., transgenic plants) of substantial commercial value.

Cases decided in the early 1980s [e.g., *Diamond* v. *Chakrabarty*, 206 U.S.P.Q. 193 (1980) and *Ex parte Hibberd*, 227 U.S.P.Q. 443 (BOPAI, 1985)] have made it clear that such developments in the biological sciences are protectable in the USA under the utility patent law. Most companies recognize that it is very important to facilitate the rapid development of plant biotechnology by making biological material available to public sector laboratories under conditions which do not undermine, or encumber the commercial goal of providing valued products to the marketplace. Hence, this led to a need to consider the framework under which biological materials were being released so as to not jeopardize the prospects for protecting the disclosing party's, patentable inventions, or in the case of entities endeavoring to develop commercial products, not to jeopardize that commercialization by facilitating patentable improvements or new inventions by recipients of the released biological materials unless such developments are accessible by license.

Since the early 1980s, Monsanto Company has, as have other companies, embraced a relatively open program for the release of biological materials such as genes, transformation vectors, and expression cassettes to public sector laboratories. Material release agreements are essential to document the conditions under which these materials are being transferred. It has been suggested that material release agreements may be of little benefit in view of the resource commitment needed to administer them. Requests for biological materials may actually be declining in view of the administrative hassle and the ability of the researchers to now re-isolate the genetic material (i.e., plant genes, bacterial genes, plant promoters, etc.) given the detail of today's scientific publications coupled with the remarkable advancements in laboratory techniques. However, it remains prudent for anyone charged with the responsibility of generating ''profits'' from research and development activities (i) to not unduly generate competition by providing products to the marketplace, and furthermore, (ii) to know as early as possible what the costs will be for using biological materials or technology acquired from another. These are the two points which are the most important points to be addressed in material release agreements.

The principle considerations to be made in a decision to release biological material are (i) the status of applications for intellectual property rights, (ii) the scope of permitted use by the recipient (i.e., use for research purposes only), (iii) whether the recipient has an existing licensing obligation to a third party, and (iv) whether an option is available to license commercially useful embodiments or improvements produced by the recipient using the biological material. The impact of the recipients work on intellectual property rights can be both positive and negative.

Most countries outside the USA require absolute novelty for patentability. That is, if one discloses or otherwise makes the material available to another the right to patent protection on that biological material is forfeited. This aspect must be weighed in a decision to release material particularly for ex-U.S. rights. However, the use of the released biological material by another laboratory may actually enure to the benefit of the patent applicant if it supports the teaching of the patent specification in another plant system. The affect of the recipient's work on later filed continuation-in-part applications must also be considered. Access to commercially-useful embodiments or improvements is the primary incentive for a company to release biological material to an outside laboratory. Essentially the same considerations are made in deciding whether to accept biological material from an outside source. In this case, the primary considerations are (i) whether there exists a pending patent application claiming the subject biological material, and (ii) the license fee for commercial use of the biological material.

Most releases of biological material by Monsanto are to laboratories in the USA, although an increasing number of requests from ex-U.S. laboratories indicate a rapidly increasing expertise in genetic engineering of plants. Monsanto has participated in a few out-reach programs where biological material and laboratory training has been provided to foreign scientists with the specific intent to facilitate the scientific and commercial use of the products of this research in the ex-U.S. country. For example, Monsanto has been involved in a cooperative effort with the U.S. Agency for International Development in which, Florence Wambugu, a research scientist from the Kenya Agricultural Research Institute, is working in Monsanto laboratories under a 3-year fellowship. Dr. Wambugu's work is directed to genetically engineering African root crops such as cassava, sweet potatoes, and yams to be resistant to viral pathogens. Another project is directed toward the development of virus resistance in peppers for use in Mexico.

15 Ethical and Social Issues of Protection

Lawrence Busch

Department of Sociology
Michigan State University
East Lansing, MI

Until very recently most agricultural research on plants was conducted exclusively by the public sector (Kloppenburg, 1988). The Plant Patent Act of 1930 (35 U.S.C. §§ 161–164) was the first law to extend intellectual property protection to plants. However, it was confined to asexually reproduced plants and in practice it was confined largely to flowers and certain fruits. The passage of the Plant Variety Protection Act (PVPA) of 1970 (7 U.S.C. § 2321 et seq.) extended intellectual property protection to plant *varieties*. The act was soon followed by a restructuring of the commercial seed industry as small seed companies were purchased by large chemical and pharmaceutical companies. More recently, the 1980 Supreme Court decision, *Diamond* v. *Chakrabarty* (447 U.S. 303), and the 1985 ruling by the U.S. Board of Patent Appeals and Interferences in *Ex parte Hibberd* [227 U.S.P.Q. (BNA) 443] granted utility patents for plants and plant parts. This dramatic expansion of intellectual property rights and the concomitant development of plant molecular biology promise to make plant improvement into a very profitable enterprise. However, at the same time, the extension of intellectual property rights, and especially utility patents, to plants raises a number of ethical and social issues (Buttel and Belsky, 1987).

NOVELTY

Many would argue that the creation of *new* living things by people involves not an invention, but a discovery. Therefore, plant breeding involves not the invention of a new organism but the discovery of an organism or variety that has certain particularly desirable properties. In conventional breeding, the methods are well established and the material is well known; what is novel is the particular combination of genes that the breeder has managed to put together, through a good deal of hard work, in a given variety.

 Intellectual Property Rights: Protection of Plant Materials, CSSA Special Publication no. 21.

Moreover, the breeder, more likely than not, is unable to explain precisely how the variety was created. Hence, there is no clearly defined process or product to patent; instead, there is a concrete object (the genetic makeup of which is far from fully understood) called a variety. Thus, many would argue that plants should be excluded from utility patenting as they are not cases of invention.

LIMITS TO PROPERTY RIGHTS

In all societies, property rights are restricted to certain categories of things. For example, in all nations the sale of human body parts is illegal. Similarly, most Americans still feel uncomfortable with the idea of patenting an animal, although owning one is generally not problematic. Some would argue that life is sacrosanct and should never be considered the property of anyone. Note that the issue here is *not* that individual organisms should not be owned, but that no variety or species should be the property of anyone. Moreover, in all societies certain things are not for sale at any price; for example, the Statue of Liberty, the Mona Lisa, and the Great Pyramid are not for sale at any price.

FLOW OF SCIENTIFIC INFORMATION

It has also been argued that the granting of utility patents for plants restricts the flow of scientific information and technical change and therefore is contrary to the intent of intellectual property rights legislation (e.g., Berlan and Lewontin, 1986; Mody, 1990). In other words, intellectual property rights involve a bargain between the inventor and society in which the inventor is rewarded with monopoly rights during a fixed period in return for full disclosure of the knowledge embodied in the invention. However, as patent rights move closer to the basic end of the research continuum, thereby blurring the very distinction between basic and applied, they tend to limit what scientists will reveal to their colleagues (Nelkin, 1984; Eisenberg, 1987). Furthermore, unlike scientific journal articles which reveal as much as possible, patent claims tend to reveal only that which is clearly required by law.

ENCOURAGING INVENTION

While the patent system was initially designed to encourage invention, it now more often serves to reduce competition, by permitting a few firms to capture certain technical areas.[1] This point was driven home in a recent study of the vacuum tube industry at the turn of the century (Reich, 1985). In that study it was noted how two companies, General Electric and AT&T, used patents to block competitors from entry and to divide the market between them. It may be argued by analogy that the large chemical and pharmaceutical companies will soon capture control over the basic patents necessary to plant improvement driving their smaller competitors out of the market. It should be noted that already many biotechnology companies have been either purchased by larger companies or have failed.

DEMOCRATIC PARTICIPATION

Unlike Europe, in the USA the decisions to include plants under the system of utility patents have been made entirely by the courts.[2] Hence, the democratic debate that would normally precede a change of this magnitude has not taken place. This leaves us with a patent law that is ill-suited for the special characteristics of living materials. Furthermore, inclusion of plants within both utility patent law and PVPA permits double protection and is fraught with contradictions (see Krosin, 1985).

THE PUBLIC GOOD

A key issue that is often occluded by the intellectual property rights (IPR debate is the unequal ability to use germplasm for the public good (Juma, 1989). Whether germplasm is defined as (private) property or not, only a handful of Third World nations (e.g., India, Brazil, Mexico) have sufficiently large research systems to use those materials effectively. Few such nations have the trained scientists needed to create new varieties; hence stronger intellectual property laws are hardly likely to spur indigenous invention. Moreover, given the relatively weak inroads that the multinational hybrid seed industry has made in the developing world, there is little reason to believe that stronger intellectual property laws will increase investment in developing nations either.

---

[1]Though many studies have been conducted, there is little evidence to suggest that the patent system actually accomplishes its task. Taylor and Silberston (1973) concluded that patents in Britain only work in a few areas including crop protection and specialty chemicals. Similarly, Levin et al. (1987) note that only a small number of R&D directors in a few industries saw patents as more important than lead time, secrecy, and the steepness of the learning curve.

[2]For an examination of the European situation see International Coalition for Development Action (1989) and Hermitte and Joly (1991). The Canadian situation is explained in Belcher and Hawtin (1991).

ATTRIBUTION OF ORIGIN

Rarely are landraces attributable to an individual, a particular time, or specific location. Similarly, today, many new varieties are the product of a *corporate* endeavor and are not truly traceable to a single breeder. Thus, when discussing Plant Breeders' Rights we are talking about the rights of a corporate entity, while in the case of Farmers' Rights we are concerned with farmers *as a class*. Neither position speaks for or against the notion of compensation. That is to say, compensation for the tasks undertaken may be provided in the form of payment to either a corporate entity or to a class. In the former case, it is relatively easy to pay royalties to a seed company, for example. In the latter, however, there is no reason why payment to nations in the form of help in conserving germplasm and *building effective plant breeding programs* cannot be carried out. Put another way, there is no reason why free access must mean access without compensation (Kloppenburg, 1990).

UNIVERSITY-GOVERNMENT RELATIONS

The extension of IPR, and especially utility patents, to plants also brings many pitfalls to university and government research on plants (Busch et al., 1991; Kenney, 1986). In particular, university and government researchers may retreat from direct contact with farmers. They may erroneously assume that the interests of the input sector are identical to those of farmers. For example, while chemical companies may wish to increase their sales of farm inputs by developing seed-chemical packages, farmers may prefer new varieties that reduce the use of other inputs and put greater control in the farmer's hands. As public servants university and government scientists must continue to balance the needs and desires of many diverse and competing groups.

UNIFORMITY IN THE FIELD

It has been argued that extension of utility patents to plants is likely to encourage greater uniformity in the field as breeders respond to legal rather than agronomic or scientific breeding requirements. For example, the uniformity and stability required by PVPA is not connected to agronomic needs. An analogy to the auto industry is appropriate. Henry Ford is said to have remarked that you could have any color Ford as long as it was black. In contrast, Sloan of General Motors opened the door to endless variations on the same theme. Similarly, the new biotechnologies may give the *appearance* of diversity while encouraging more product differentiation. Moreover, even the registrations under the PVPA have been limited to just a few widely grown crops and there is no evidence to suggest that any significant increase in overall R&D occurred as a result of that law (Council for Agricultural Science and Technology, 1985). Smaller markets, for many fruit and vegetable crops, for example, may well be ignored as the cost of research outweighs the profits to be derived by both the private and public sectors.

In sum, the new forms of intellectual property rights for plants raise numerous complex social and ethical issues. We would do well to pause to reflect before rushing headlong into the thicket of issues before us.

REFERENCES

Belcher, B., and G. Hawtin. 1991. A patent on life: Ownership of plant and animal research. Intl Development Res. Centre, Ottawa.

Berlan, J.-P., and R. Lewontin. 1986. Breeders' rights and patenting life forms. Nature (London) 322:785–788.

Busch, L., W.B. Lacy, J. Burkhardt, and L. R. Lacy. 1991. Plants, power, and profit: Social, economic, and ethical consequences of the new biotechnologies. Basil Blackwell, Cambridge, MA.

Buttel, F. H., and J. Belsky. 1987. Biotechnology, plant breeding, and intellectual property: Social and ethical dimensions. Sci. Technol. Human Values. 12:31–49.

Council for Agricultural Science and Technology. 1985. Plant germplasm preservation and utilization in U.S. agriculture. CAST Report no. 106. Ames, IA.

Eisenberg, R.S. 1987. Proprietary rights and the norms of science in biotechnology. Yale Law J. 97:177–231.

Hermitte, M.-A., and P.-B. Joly. 1991. Biotechnologies et brevets: Presentation des differents modèles juridiques et analyse de leur impact sur la dynamique de l'innovation dans les industries des semences. Université des Sciences Sociales, Grenoble, France.

International Coalition for Development Action. 1989. Patenting life forms in Europe. Proc. of a Conference at the European Parliament. Brussels.

Juma, C. 1989. The gene hunters: Biotechnology and the scramble for seeds. Princeton Univ. Press, Princeton, NJ.

Kenney, M. 1986. Biotechnology: The university-industrial complex. Yale Univ. Press, New Haven, CT.

Kloppenburg, J.R., Jr. 1988. First the seed: The political economy of plant biotechnology, 1492–2000. Cambridge Univ. Press, New York.

Kloppenburg, J.R. 1990. No hunting! Scientific poaching and global biodiversity. Z Mag. (September):104–108.

Krosin, K.E. 1985. Are plants patentable under the utility patent act? J. Pat. Off. Soc. 67:220–238.

Levin, R.C., A.K. Klevorick, R.R. Nelson, and S.G. Winter. 1987. Appropriating the returns from industrial research and development. Brookings Papers on Economic Activity. 3:783–820.

Mody, A. 1990. New international environment for intellectual property rights. p. 203–239. *In* F.W. Rushing and C.G. Brown (ed.) Intellectual property rights in science, technology, and economic performance. Westview Press, Boulder, CO.

Nelkin, D. 1984. Science and technology policy and the democratic process. p. 18–39. *In* J.C. Petersen (ed.) Citizen participation in science policy. Univ. of Massachusetts Press, Amherst.

Reich, L.S. 1985. The making of american industrial research: Science and business at GE and Bell, 1876–1926. Cambridge Univ. Press, Cambridge, England.

Taylor, C.T., and Z.A. Silberston. 1973. The economic impact of the patent system: A study of British experience. Cambridge Univ. Press, Cambridge, England.

16 The Impact of Intellectual Property Protection on the Private Research Agenda

Keith A. Walker

Mycogen Corp.,
San Diego, CA

By its very nature, the private sector is focused on the development of proprietary rights in its developed technology. Historically, companies involved in the seed trade sought to protect their proprietary technology by the development of hybrid varieties of crop plants which could not be reproduced without ready access to the parent lines. The importance of intellectual property protection as a part of an overall business strategy has always been part of private sector thinking, granting that enterprises have differed in the focus of their research dollars and product development energies, which may have been based on factors other than the particular advantage one species may have by virtue of its reproducive system.

In the USA, the lack of proprietary rights protection created two classes of crops. The first tier, where technology investments were almost always encouraged and research spending as a percentage of sales was relatively high; and all others, where R&D investments were given careful consideration in terms of the cost-versus-return possibilities and where technology always lagged behind. Examples of the former are vegetables, ornamentals, and corn. Examples of the latter are soybean and many of the cereal grains. With the extension of utility patent rights to cover novel plant inventions, the enthusiasm for the investment in new technology in these "second class" crops is on the rise.

In international markets, where strong breeder's rights and varietal registration are possible, companies have more aggressively invested in non-hybrid crop development. In those jurisdictions where no rights were available, alternative strategies recognizing the early loss of proprietary rights are the norm (e.g., joint ventures with local enterprises to control technology, foundation seed sales approaches, and up-front payment strategies.)

In short, since the private sector has had to develop a variety of approaches to crop commercialization based on proprietary rights issues, R&D

programs have had to mirror that diversity. One potential impact of this is the loss of R&D dollar cost efficiency in breeding and technology development programs. Perhaps the most significant impact of strengthened and ''normalized'' intellectual property rights around the world can be in the cost efficiencies which it brings to the product development process.

As regards public-private interactions, the enthusiasm to seek proprietary rights in intellectual property on the part of many in the public sector is creating great opportunities for the future. A challenge in conducting business with the public sector is that the public sector generally seeks license fees, research support, and/or royalties for its technology. Whereas, in the private sector technology transactions may include marketing rights, joint R&D and cost sharing, and cash-neutral technology exchange in addition to licensing fees and royalties as part of an overall relationship. As a consequence, it is often easier to find a shared interest with a private concern which facilitates a transaction.

17 Intellectual Property Rights: Protection of Plant Materials Public Research Agendas

Charles E. Hess

University of California
Davis, CA

As stated in the Office of Technology Assessment report, *New Developments in Biotechnology: Patenting Life*, intellectual property protection in the USA has its origin in the U.S. Constitution (Art. I; Sec. 8; U.S. Congress, Office of Technology Assessment, 1989). It provides Congress the power to "promote the Progress of Science and the useful Arts, by securing for limited Times to Authors and Inventors the exclusive right to their respective Writings and Discoveries." Congress enacted the first patent and copyright laws in 1790. Intellectual property protection serves multiple purposes. It encourages inventiveness by granting to researchers a limited property right, and at the same time, requires the inventor to describe the invention in sufficient detail that a knowledgeable person could make use of the invention. In most universities the concept of providing an incentive to discover and file for a patent has been followed by the university retaining patent rights but providing the inventor a percentage of the royalties. The requirement to disclose the details of the patent ensures that useful knowledge is not kept secret, which might slow research in a field or lead to duplication of work already completed. However, this provision may not be important in a university environment where there already exist plenty of incentives to publish. These are meritorious objectives that facilitate technology transfer and help maintain the nation's competitiveness, important issues in view of the nation's current economic environment. Perhaps less meritorious, but still viewed as positive, is the possibility that intellectual property protection will also create a stream of income for the university, department, and/or researcher's laboratory which will help offset decreases in the public support of research.

Unfortunately, as with most well meaning policies, there are also costs which should be taken into account. Few things in life are win-win, and one of the challenges for policy makers is to be sure that (i) the costs are

---

 Intellectual Property Rights: Protection of Plant Materials, CSSA Special Publication no. 21.

considered and evaluated with the benefits and, that (ii) they develop a policy which maximizes the benefits and minimizes the costs.

What are some of the costs that should be taken into consideration? Perhaps the greatest cost is that intellectual property rights and the potential to generate income from them will result in a decrease in the informal flow and exchange of information. Certainly, a significant discovery will be published or patented, but much of the progress made in science comes from the free exchange of ideas, which occurs well before a discovery ends up in a new process or product. A forum for this, in addition to daily interactions among faculty, is the exchange that takes place at scientific meetings. It has been suggested, however, that the flow of new, unpublished information has slowed appreciably at plant biotechnology meetings and that presenters have achieved new levels of evasiveness in response to questions.

In a similar vein, and of particular importance to plant breeding, is the willingness to exchange germplasm. As the potential for receiving income from protecting a new variety increases, the willingness to exchange germplasm decreases. Certainly, in the international arena we have seen that the accessibility of germplasm has decreased, or at least the cost of obtaining it has increased; in part, this is because of a greater appreciation of its value. This is an important ''cost'' for the USA, since most of our cultivated plants have their origins in other parts of the world. This is particularly important as we seek genetic resistance to insects and disease as an alternative to pesticides in sustainable agricultural systems. The potential for further increasing the value of a new variety through utility patents exacerbates the problem of international germplasm exchange and the demands for payment of unimproved germplasm will likely increase. ''Farmer rights,'' or the concept of rewarding farmers in less developed nations for preserving and selecting germplasm, has been a contentious issue in international negotiations on germplasm.

The potential for limiting access to germplasm is not limited to international exchange. While I was in the USDA as Assistant Secretary for Science and Education, we received a request from an experiment station not to distribute any seed from the National Seed Storage laboratory that had been submitted by its breeders. Another example of decreased accessibility is the concern that utility patents will inhibit the process in which traditional advances are made in plant breeding. In the past, when a breeder developed a new variety with better disease resistance, it was introduced into the market. Other breeders used that variety to make further improvements such as adapting it to a different climate. In this way, there was an incremental improvement in U.S. crops. Now, with the utility patent, a breeder can exclude others from using a protected variety to develop new varieties. It is also possible to protect a specific genetic trait across varieties, such as a specific oil content in all sunflower varieties, even those yet to be developed. It has been stated ''. . .that the biological domain was once public domain but has shifted to private property right (U.S. Congress, Office of Technology Assessment, 1989, p.87)."

With the current budgetary crunch hitting most universities, there is increased pressure from administrators to seek new sources of funding. There are some examples of patents which have been important sources of income. The patenting of Warfarin and the process to increase the Vitamin D content of milk by the Wisconsin Alumni Research Foundation at Madison are examples. With the advent of biotechnology, other examples can be identified. Therefore, intellectual property rights have increased in importance as potential sources of support. The concern is that there will be pressure on faculty to pursue research that is more market-oriented. The potential shift away from more fundamental research is exacerbated by the current congressional pressures on agencies such as the National Science Foundation to do research that is more relevant to social problems and to pay more attention to technology transfer. Establishing the balance between basic and applied research is always a challenge, and the externalities that are influencing this balance are on the increase, currently placing increased emphasis on market-directed research.

Although there is a gleam in the eyes of administrators and some faculty about the potential to generate substantial income for their institution or laboratory, the big gainers are few and far between. The costs of the patent offices, and the lawyers associated with them, often consume the royalties that are realized. If, in fact, substantial royalty funds are realized, it is not always a blessing. An unhealthy competition for the funds often develops. The investigator receives part of the royalty because of his or her intellectual contributions to the discovery. However, in public institutions, funded by tax dollars, there is often a question raised about what is the appropriate percentage that should go to the inventor since it can be argued that many people contribute directly and indirectly to an invention. On the other hand, if the return is not substantial, there will be no incentive to deal with all the red tape associated with getting a patent. Then an argument arises among the other actors in the university infrastructure. The university, college, and department all want their share. In publicly supported universities, the legislators may feel that it is possible to cut back on the state's contribution of tax funds when there are substantial royalties, just as back on the state's contribution of tax funds when there are substantial royalties, just as many states do in taking their share of indirect costs. It can end up in a zero-sum gain.

A new dimension of this debate has taken shape in recent years. In cases where commodity groups provide financial support via marketing orders or other forms of industry support to help the development of new varieties, these groups also want a share of the royalties. In some cases there are negotiations for part of the potential royalties at the time the research contract is developed. The end result is the potential for a lot of bad relations, often over a relatively small amount of money. The most important impact of the increased pressure for royalty income, however, is the potential to shift the research agenda toward the applied end of the basic-to-applied research continuum. Finally, the emphasis on intellectual property rights and the potential to create wealth has helped create an environment which erodes scientific integrity. Science is not pursued for scientific merits, but for money. The end result can be that the university and its scientists lose credibility (Kline, 1989).

It may well be that the overall public good from the current intellectual property right policy justifies the costs. However, that judgement should be made on a fully informed basis.

REFERENCES

U.S. Congress, Office of Technology Assessment. 1989. New developments in biotechnology: Patenting life—special report. OTA-BA-370. U.S. Gov. Print. Office, Washington, DC.

Kline, A. D. 1989. Bioethics—Impact of proprietary rights in public research goals. p. 25-34. *In* B.E. Caldwell et al. (ed.) Intellectual property rights associated with plants. ASA Spec. Publ. 52. CSSA, ASA, and SSSA, Madison, WI.

Workgroup Reports

Workgroup A: Licensing

Licensing is important to both the public and private sectors as a primary vehicle by which intellectual property rights (IPR) are transferred from the inventor to the farmer and consumer. Licensing in the USA is flexible in form and content, and is essentially unregulated despite its public importance. Licensing agreements are generally private, contractual, negotiated, and differ on a case-by-case basis, depending on the technologies and parties involved.

The private sector is generally comfortable with the application of IPR to plants and the licensing of plant IPR. However, there is significant uncertainty in evaluating the usefulness, technical feasibility, and value of individual plant inventions. Uncertainty in assessing usefulness often causes difficulties in negotiating a license in the early research and development stages. This uncertainty has led to the use of Material Transfer Agreements (MTAs) as one type of licensing agreement which often allows only research activities with the transferred material. Under the terms of these agreements, if a new commercial product is developed subsequently, the owner may reserve the right to grant a license for commercial sale and use, or leave the critical terms of a license arrangement (particularly the royalties) to later negotiation and agreement.

The value of plant intellectual property, and who will share in that value, are still uncertain; however, product development continues at a great pace. These issues will sort themselves out in a competitive marketplace.

ISSUES

Public Licensing Practices. To facilitate dissemination of information and to evaluate potential licensing arrangements, it is important to have consistent and organized licensing practices at public institutions. Public institutions need to be better organized and more business-like when handling new inventions and their licensing. For example, to assist in making quicker decisions, institutions should define how licensing decisions are made, and by whom. Preferably, these decisions should be made by one individual or office, rather than by committee. Often, private companies do not know who to deal with in the university and are uninformed as to when inventions are available. Also, to be able to offer a basis for licensing and potential commercialization, public institutions must preserve their rights in intellectual property and personal property.

Exclusivity. Exclusive license agreements create tensions with regard to (i) access to germplasm, and (ii) return on investment. It is important to use MTAs whenever possible to clarify the intent of the parties involved. MTAs should be well written, and must be tailored to a specific case-by-case basis.

Guidelines for writing MTAs are needed which include several examples. The Breeder's Exchange Agreement under the "Code of Ethics for Germplasm Exchange" may be useful in certain circumstances for defining these guidelines.

Equitable Treatment of Breeders. Unequal treatment of plant breeders as inventors among public and private institutions is perceived as a serious problem. This issue has clear ethical and social ramifications. No consensus was found, but a majority of work group members felt it is important to encourage a consistent policy within and among organizations. Certain State laws may mandate royalties in a specific fashion for plant breeders.

Within a public institution only certain crop species have the potential and/or opportunity to generate significant revenue. This causes inequity of royalty opportunity within and among departments. It is, thus, important to recognize that a new product is most likely the result of a team effort; and it is important to treat plant breeders or plant breeding teams in a manner similar to inventors in other technologies, such as mechanical engineering, electrical engineering, or chemistry. A consistent policy among departments should be encouraged. Who is the inventor? This can be determined by a "proportionate creativity" equation, e.g., a person making the initial breeding cross receives x% of the ultimate ownership, the pathologist receives x%, the entomologist receives x%, and so forth, where each percentage depends on the contribution to the final product.

A comparison of the policies from several public institutions represented within the work group showed that currently from 25 to 50% of any profit goes directly to the individual inventor. Possibly, the Experiment Station Committee on Organization and Policy (ESCOP) could discuss this variable percentage to the inventor and come to some consensus about the issue.

A third area in which there is compensatory inconsistency of breeders as inventors is in private companies. Private breeders generally do not receive a bonus or percent of any profit; however, they may receive other deferred compensations based on their productivity.

Public Funds and Exclusive Licenses. What is the effect of licensing, especially exclusive licenses, on the credibility of public organizations in the eyes of the general public? Public funds have partially or fully paid for the research; however, commercial products which are generated by this research are often exclusively licensed to private interests.

It is very important for public institutions to ensure equal access to any protected material; otherwise, there is a potential problem of bias--be it perceived or real. It is important that the public be apprised of the entire situation. Licensing procedures should include broad-based notification of all technology when it becomes available. It must be assumed that the press will examine all institutional decisions. The goal must be to maximize public benefit; revenue should not be the highest priority.

Factors to consider when licensing a new invention include (i) public trust, (ii) duty to the public at large, (iii) duty to taxpayers, and (iv) duty to the inventor to protect the invention.

Education and Communication. Education and communication about licensing issues should be improved. The private perspective is that public institutions should set a clear policy and then follow through. Universities also need to inform new faculty and staff about licensing, MTAs, and IPR in general. Networking is an important way for different groups to share what has worked for them. The bottom line regarding education and communication is ''JUST DO IT!''

Material Transfer Agreements. An important form of an initial license agreement is the MTA, which may have a clause stating that any use is for ''research purposes only.'' This agreement affects ownership rights in future new products. Public institutions need to develop the capacity to negotiate with others in a ''business-like fashion.'' It is important to retain some flexibility for future developments.

License Enforcement. Licenses must be enforced when there is a breach of a license by the licensee, e.g., (i) non ''due diligence'' by a licensee who is not marketing the product adequately, or (ii) when the licensee gives materials to unauthorized third parties. Licenses are ineffective unless they are enforced. The State Attorney General's office often can be helpful in enforcement.

Essentially Derived Varieties. The concept of ''essentially derived varieties'' (EDV) should be defined and put into a license agreement. A mutually agreed upon definition of EDV could avoid later disagreements on ownership rights (see Appendix 2, p. 159).

CONCLUDING REMARKS

Emerging opportunities for new plant innovations, including specialty crops and improved cultivars, are creating (i) new business opportunities for industry and public institutions, and (ii) new strategies for the transfer of university technology for public advantage. To justify private sector investment and to be able to offer a basis for licensing and potential commercialization, the university must preserve its rights (in personal property, as well as intellectual property). If options are maintained through the use of MTAs and filing for patent and plant breeding rights, an appropriate license will be possible.

At this time, most universities want to undertake licensing programs, but many are not implementing policies to generate and retain the rights which support the licensing. We urge that cooperative educational efforts be undertaken through workshops, invited speakers, American Society of Agronomy publications, and other avenues to enhance university understanding of the role of property rights and strategies to protect these rights. In addition, it is anticipated that industry generally would be willing to provide information on business development and marketing strategies to ensure fair valuation of opportunities by all parties. While university practices need not be uniform, licensing discussion are greatly enhanced by adherence to at least internally consistent practices.

Workgroup B: Exemptions

Farmer and research exemptions vary with the type of plant intellectual property rights (IPR) protection. There is no provision for either of these exemptions under the U.S. Plant Patent Act of 1930, which grants IPR protection for asexually propagated plants except tubers. However, the Plant Variety Protection Act (PVPA) of 1970, which covers sexually reproduced plants, contains provisions for both exemptions. The PVPA farmer exemption has been the subject of considerable debate and litigation. The research exemption may be of little practical consequence because there is no requirement that seed of the protected variety be made available; so, while research with the variety is allowed, the seed required to conduct the research may not be available.

Utility patent laws make no provision for exemptions. Such patents are much harder to get and more costly than Plant Variety Protection (PVP) certificates. Therefore, substantially more complete protection seems reasonable. There has never been any sustained effort to establish a farmer exemption for utility patents. Some movement toward research exemptions, more specifically experimental-use exemptions, has occurred through judicial decisions. These appear to provide precedent for exemption from infringement penalties for "non-commercial" research. The difficulty arises in defining "non-commercial."

Previously, research at university and U.S. government laboratories was considered non-commercial. However, for reasons cited below, university and U.S. government laboratories are showing more and more interest in the commercial potential of their research. Because of this trend, industrial representatives are insisting that the commercial activities of all researchers, whether they work in commercial, academic, or U.S. government laboratories, ought to be governed by the same rules. Concurrently, there is a perception by some university and U.S. government researchers that a potential exists for future problems with regard to access to germplasm and other technology for research. Conversely, where such access is available, a problem is seen in the commercialization of results arising from research which uses the protected technology of others.

ISSUES

Farmer Exemption. The PVPA not only allows a farmer to save protected seed for his or her own use, but also to sell surplus seed to a neighbor. Unfortunately, the word "neighbor" has in some instances been very loosely interpreted with resulting financial harm to the PVP certificate holder.

This issue is now before us because there is a need to amend the PVPA to make it conform to the International Union for the Protection of New

Varieties of Plants (UPOV) Convention of 1991. There seems to be general agreement that the farmer exemption under the PVPA should not be made broader than the position adopted by the 1992 American Farm Bureau Federation Resolution Committee Report:

> "We will . . . (3) Support restricting sales of protected varieties, except for incidental sales, without the permission of the owner."

The key to this position is the meaning of "incidental." For example, there seems to be general acceptance of the proposition that farmers should be permitted to sell seed with which they are "stuck," in the event they are growing under contract with the variety owner and the latter defaults on obligations to purchase the seed. On the other hand, the exemption should be tightened to eliminate abuses with crops for which the seed is not normally harvested, such as leaf and root vegetables and alfalfa.

Minimum Distance and Essentially Derived Varieties. If a new variety is created through research, and it is derived in part from a variety protected under the PVPA, how different must the new variety be to be awarded a PVP certificate? This required difference is called "minimum distance" by PVPA office, and is the subject of much debate. Many plant breeders believe the applied minimum difference standards are too narrow. This narrowness permits a distinct variety to be protected even though it is sufficiently close to its parent and should reasonably fall within the enforceable scope of the parent variety's certificate. The new UPOV Convention introduces the concept of "essentially derived varieties." Marketing a variety essentially derived from a protected one without a license would be an infringement. Molecular markers can be used to distinguish between varieties, but their use does not settle the issue of the level of difference required to meet minimum distance or essential derivation standards.

Free Exchange of Germplasm. Patenting of plants may conceivably interfere with free and open exchange of biological materials to be used for research, and therefore impede future genetic progress. This is a particular concern in university and U.S. government laboratories.

The problem underlying the perceived concerns is actually associated with several trends: (i) the increasing competitiveness of plant research; (ii) a perception of a proliferation of increased financial incentives for, and rewards from, successfully commercialized plant research; (iii) the reduction or erosion of university and U.S. government agricultural research budgets and the increased competition for research funds; and (iv) the use of licensable protection to provide for successful technology transfer from academic or U.S. government laboratories to the marketplace.

While concerns about access to germplasm generally are associated with the advent of plant utility patents, this association is not justified by the facts. As already mentioned, the PVPA does not require that protected seed be made available for research. Moreover, trade secrecy, contract, or bailment protection for varieties permit the restriction of access to or use of varieties on terms which are defined solely within the discretion of the owner.

One approach to allaying concerns about exchange of germplasm and information would be to make a research exemption elective under the utility patent law. In another approach, the Agricultural Research Service is suggesting consideration of a research exemption policy for products of plant research conducted or funded by the Department of Agriculture.

CONCLUDING REMARKS

With regard to the issues of farmer and research exemptions under the PVPA, the intent of any new legislation needs to be established as clearly as possible through the accompanying legislative record. The importance of the research exemption for university and U.S. government researchers is underscored by the fact that it is addressed in three of the four other work group reports (Information Exchange, Social and Ethical Issues, and Research Agenda). In the case of utility patents, there is a de facto exemption for "pure" research because of its minimal commercial impact and the high cost of patent litigation. The latter makes enforcement financially prohibitive unless the research has a clear commercial objective and potential for harming the financial interests of the patent holder. There have been instances of companies, especially small new ones, trying to prevent research with their patented plants through intimidating letters. On the other hand, there probably is much more actual infringement (commercially oriented research) on patented plants than is generally known. More education is needed for both the public sector researchers to find out what is patented and what they can and cannot do with patented materials, and for companies to consider limitations, legal and practical, which they should try to place on research use of their patented material.

New legislation might be needed to enable the USDA to require that any USDA patents be subject to a research exemption. There might be serious opposition to such a change in the law. Alternatively, language in the 1990 Farm Bill authorizing the Plant Genome Program might be interpreted as providing a basis for a research exemption policy to be implemented administratively. A research exemption could legitimately be requested in negotiations for grants.

Workgroup C: Germplasm and Information Exchange

The goal of germplasm and information exchange is to make the best genetic resources available for use in world agriculture. Even though surpluses exist for many crop commodities today, the doubling of the world's population by the middle of the next century will drastically increase the demand for these commodities. Effective and efficient systems for exchange of germplasm and information are essential for meeting the required genetic gains for many of these world food crops.

For the purposes of this discussion, germplasm is broadly defined and includes all genetic materials and information associated with plants such as landraces, advanced breeding lines, varieties, cloned genes, probes, and nucleotide sequences.

Exchanges range from the very formal and legally enforceable types to those that are more informal and not legally enforceable. Formal exchanges are be characterized by explicit expectations such as various forms of licenses (i.e., Material Transfer Agreements). The informal type is represented by exchange among scientists where no stated expectations exist. This type includes exchanges with most public germplasm banks. Free exchange means the exchange is unrestricted in nature; whereas, exchange for free means that no costs are associated with the exchange. By definition, exchange requires more than one party and that each makes a contribution (in this case, information or germplasm). Ideally, exchanges should be quid pro quo (equally reciprocal exchanges), but realistically this is hard to implement because of the difficulty in assigning value to germplasm and information.

It should be recognized that all germplasm contains intellectual property, and its ownership is a key issue in determining protection and licensing opportunities. This is an important consideration for the world's gene banks and their obligations for free, unrestricted exchanges. In the international agriculture research system called the Consultative Group for International Agriculture Research (CGIAR), for example, the germplasm resources held in banks are considered to belong to the world's people and the international research centers are simply acting as trustees.

Living plant germplasm is unique, and different from other types of intellectual property in which patents can be obtained. Higher plant germplasm is difficult to describe verbally and impossible to duplicate from a verbal description. In contrast to most other types of intellectual property, germplasm improvement research requires physical access to the germplasm itself and not just a description.

There are several pertinent issues associated with enhancement of plant germplasm exchange and preservation. For scientist-to-scientist exchanges, exchange of germplasm in amounts sufficient to ensure future genetic gains should be encouraged. The following are recommendations designed to promote this germplasm flow: (i) encourage the use of research exemptions for public sector agriculture utility patents for plants, (ii) encourage the amendment of the U.S. Plant Variety Protection Act of 1970 to include the concept of "essentially derived varieties" and promote the use of this type of protection for most general purpose germplasm, and (iii) encourage policies which guarantee that the products of agricultural molecular biology from public programs have the same unrestricted exchange as do the more traditional germplasm products. For country-to-country exchanges, germplasm exchanges should be unrestricted. Currently, however, bi- and multi-lateral agreements occur and probably will continue in the future. Finally, mechanisms need to be defined by which restricted-use germplasm is preserved and distributed. This would ensure the public availability of restricted-use germplasm when the protection no longer applies. The American Type Culture Collection performs this function today, but an additional mechanism is needed (such as inclusion in the National Seed Storage Laboratory after a certain time limit).

The following are educational needs pertaining to patents on plant genetic material and their effects on germplasm exchange which should be addressed. Students in agriculture need to have an understanding of intellectual property rights regarding plants. General information on plant germplasm patents should be incorporated into curricula. Information on procedures for obtaining access to genetic resources in public gene banks should be widely distributed. The scientific and lay community need to be aware of the unrestricted access of these resources. University faculty and administrators need to know more about the various types of intellectual property protection and the implications for germplasm exchange and how intellectual property rights can affect the availability of germplasm.

Workgroup D: Ethical and Social Issues of Protection

POLICY RECOMMENDATIONS

The work group recommends six policy initiatives that result from an evaluation of seven major ethical or social concerns about plant intellectual property right (IPR) protection.

1. Educate students and the general public on the ethical dimensions of current plant IPR issues. This education would foster rational discussion and decisions on the value of policies as they are being developed. Students would benefit from participatory evaluation and guidance in research ethics.
2. Merge or rewrite the present plant IPR laws to foster the development of plant IPR instruments uniformly applicable to protection of all types of plant IPR.
3. Develop a research exemption policy that maximizes and facilities breeder access to germplasm worldwide. This policy would include contractual arrangements between private parties and between private and public entities.
4. Develop and implement an arbitration mechanism to resolve disputes on plant IPR, with leadership from the research and education community. Resolving disputes in the courts on these issues between various institutions will be extremely expensive.
5. Foster continued public funding and quasi-public funding of research in the public sector. Consortia, commodity groups, and other non-profit organizations should be encouraged to finance and support public sector research. This is important in minimizing perceptions of impropriety stemming from direct (one-to-one) relationships between public agencies and private companies.
6. Develop appropriate policies to provide just compensation to developing nations for the use of germplasm obtained from within their borders. These policies will nurture good relationships between developed and developing nations in the area of plant IPR.

The working group believes that many of the ethical and social issues that are important in plant IPR are complex and subject to varying interpretations. We agree that certain plant IPR issues have social or ethical content, but we may disagree on the nature and consequences of the issues. Nevertheless, it is important to maintain a dialogue to try to approach consensus, agreement, or at least a better understanding of contrasting views.

INTRODUCTION

The ethical and social issues of protecting plant intellectual property rights (IPR) were evaluated by considering the following set of fundamental questions: What are the principles relating to the virtues and faults of the plant IPR protection process; what are the appropriate aims of the process, who are its beneficiaries, and who does it neglect; what social goals should plant IPR protection serve; and what reasoning supports our judgments and actions on plant IPR protection? As the work group identified the important issues in plant IPR protection, they recognized that the ethical and social content of the issues are closely tied to important questions about implementation of plant IPR procedures. Ethical issues were not always independent of social issues. Nevertheless, the work group initially identified 21 ethical or social concerns about plant IPR protection. Evaluation of these issues led to the six policy recommendations.

ACCESS TO GERMPLASM

What agencies, institutions, and individuals should have access to germplasm? What are the ethical considerations of public vs. private access? Should compensation be a factor in allowing access? Should utility patents restrict access to protected plant materials for only certain types of research? Who does this restriction serve, and who does it neglect?

Present practice or policy. Several methods are available for protecting plant IPR. These methods permit genetic inventions to be treated as private property for purposes of commercialization to recover development costs and to earn a profit.

Ethical concerns. Should protection of genetic inventions be allowed when the raw materials of the invention, i.e., undeveloped germplasm, were not the private property of the inventor? Should public institutions protect plant inventions with added value? Is plant IPR protection by public institutions in the greater public interest? Should protection of plant IPR deny, for 17 or 18 years, access to the new knowledge or technology? Can the scope of claims for the invention exceed its contribution? Does plant IPR protection allow the public inventor or institution to capture "fruits of labor?"

Social concerns. Are the existing methods of protecting plant IPR adequate to capture social benefits? Who benefits from access to various methods of plant IPR protection, and who is hindered? Who decides what to count as benefits? What external costs are ignored, e.g., environmental problems, social inequities, and geopolitical inequities?

FOSTERING BIODIVERSITY

What are the present and future effects of plant IPR policies on biodiversity? Specifically, should developing nations be compensated for germplasm obtained from within their borders? If so, how?

Present practice or policy. As a nation, the USA has not officially, as of this workshop, embraced the United Nations Rio Convention on Biological Diversity. Nevertheless, material transfer agreements (MTAs) are being used as tools to foster exchange of germplasm among nations, and between private and public parties in different nations.

Ethical concerns. Are MTAs appropriate instruments for facilitating the conservation of indigenous genetic resources? Whom do they serve, and whom do they neglect? What are the appropriate forms of compensation for access to genetic resources of a developing nation, e.g., cash, forgiving indebtedness, research and development infrastructure? What are the external costs of our methods of protecting, or not protecting, plant genetic resources in developing nations? Who cares and why? Who pays? Public? Private? How does the public pay?

Social concerns. Will the use of MTAs encourage third world nations to develop their natural plant genetic resources? Will use of MTAs to exchange genetic resources increase the cost of research and development, therefore limiting rate of technology progress? Do MTAs serve the greater good of the global community?

THE PLANT AS PRIVATE PROPERTY

Should plant materials be private property? If so, how should ownership be defined? What new instruments of ownership should be developed, or are current ones appropriate?

Present practice or policy. Plants and plant genetic parts are protected as private property by law or by judicial decision.

Ethical concerns. Ownership of private property for profit-making purposes is a legitimate and primary purpose of the commercial sector. However, the profit motive is not a primary purpose of the academic sector. Is it appropriate for the academic sector, especially the public academic sector, to directly compete for profit with the commercial sector in protection and commercialization of plant IPR? Who cares and why?

Social concerns. The management of plants as private property encourages investment, increases knowledge, improves living standards, and fosters innovation. Do these practices restrict the access of some players to germplasm, narrow the research agenda, and lead to neglect of minor crops?

EFFECTS OF IPR POLICIES ON SOCIAL STRUCTURES AND AGRICULTURAL SUSTAINABILITY

What are the effects of plant IPR policies on the social structure of agriculture? Specifically, how will IPR policies affect the development of agricultural systems that are sustainable and stable?

Present practice or policy. The use of plant IPR rights is consistent with the paradigm of the market economy: maximize competitiveness and return on investment.

Ethical concerns. Does protection of plant IPR foster vertical integration in the agricultural sector and displace the farmer as the primary customer of the input industries? Who does this benefit, and who does it disadvantage? Have we adequately considered the external costs of adopting new technologies based upon plant protection? Who cares and why? What are the external costs?

Social concerns. How will increased adoption of technologies based upon plant IPR protection affect the future of the family farm? Of rural communities? Will these new technologies be better for the environment? Who has the responsibility for these issues?

SURVIVAL OF PUBLIC SECTOR RESEARCH AND DEVELOPMENT

What are the effects of plant IPR policies on the sustainability, stability, and well-being of the public sector research systems in academia and government?

Present practice or policy. Long-term investments in public sector research and development capacity are eroding. Public sector R&D is adopting a short-term vision for delivery of results. The academic sector is increasing its protection of plant IPR to secure new sources of research support. The USDA-ARS is suggesting consideration, on a case-by-case basis, the protection of plant IPR in exchange for a research exemption.

Ethical concerns. What is the justification for nonuniform implementation of plant IPR policies among academic institutions, and among units within a single academic institution? What is the justification for nonuniform application of plant IPR policies among the public university—federal government (USDA-ARS)—commercial sector participants in germplasm exchange?

exchange? Are the negative public perceptions of public university or USDA-ARS contracts with the commercial sector justified? Who cares and why?

Social concerns. Does nonstandard application of plant IPR policies cause participants or sectors to benefit unequally from advances in science and technology? Are public universities justly perceived as shirking their education mandate? Do legislatures react to perceived irresponsibility in teaching by cutting or redirecting scarce research funds? Are public universities caught up on pedaling the ''IPR treadmill'' to sustain their plant research programs?

FARMER RIGHTS

What rights should farmers retain after purchasing and growing privately developed, protected seed?

Present practice or policy. Current laws governing the use and sale of farmer-saved seed are being interpreted in the courts. The International Union for the Protection of New Varieties of Plants (UPOV) Convention is an initiative to harmonize national policies on farmer-saved seed.

Ethical concerns. Is the sale of farmer-saved seed ''counterfeiting?'' Is it equitable for the courts to penalize all growers for the transgression of a few? Whose interests are being served by prohibiting the sale of farmer-saved seed, and whose are being neglected? Who cares and why?

Social concerns. Will enforcement of laws prohibiting farmer-saved seed lead to increased input costs to the farmer, since there would be one less (class of) incentive(s) for input suppliers to be inefficient? Farmer ''abuse'' of the saved-seed privilege is blamed for abandonment of some wheat R&D programs by the commercial sector. Does farmer ''abuse'' thwart competition and reduce input choices (seed choices) that eventually become available to the producer?

EDUCATION OF STUDENTS & PUBLIC

What are the ethical considerations in educating the public about plant IPR policies and their implications?

Present practice or policy. Most graduate students learn about plant IPR protection policy and mechanisms on an ad hoc basis from their faculty mentor (advisor) or peers. Few educational institutions are revising undergraduate and graduate curricula to incorporate plant IPR knowledge. The general public receives information on plant IPR through the lay media, generally as revelations of impropriety.

Ethical concerns. As mentors with IPR knowledge, do we have a responsibility to the next generation of scientists and educators? Do we have a responsibility to be forthright with the general public?

Social concerns. Will an informed public be more likely to make intelligent and rational decisions on plant IPR policy? Will an informed student body and general public foster increased trust of science by the citizenry?

Workgroup E: Research Agendas

Research agendas at both public institutions and private companies are changing in response to current economic and legalistic pressures. Many universities now face a fiscal crisis created by the sluggish U.S. economy and other factors. There are strong pressures to use research results to generate significant revenue. The potential for income from patents could influence academic research agendas.

The availability of utility patents to protect plant varieties, genes, and crop improvement methods has created concern about competitive position in this new era of proprietary protection. Some seed companies (those whose research efforts have mostly been traditional breeding) are attempting to meet this threat by increasing research budgets or shifting resources away from traditional programs. They have also increased germplasm enhancement efforts and have started cellular and molecular biology research programs to stay competitive.

ISSUES

Income for Public Institutions

Currently, the USDA-ARS employs intellectual property rights (IPR) protection only if it enhances the potential for technology transfer, and Cooperative Research and Development Agreements are the principal mechanisms used to promote technology transfer. At universities, royalties are being collected where possible and the net income after the expenses are paid is shared by researchers, departments, and the institution.

Pressure to generate income in a period of shrinking financial resources could drive universities to excessive use of IPR to supplement support that currently comes primarily from public sources. In anticipation of the income potential for IPR, university legal staffs have been expanded and technology transfer offices have been created. In this era of diminished funding, there is growing pressure to lessen emphasis on research and to strengthen involvement with undergraduate instruction. The reliance on soft money (grants, contracts, and similar short-term funds) for support of research programs is increasing. There is pressure for colleges of agriculture to use the same criteria for distributing income from patents as the other colleges in the university. There are feelings that many institutions are not realistic and overestimate income potential and the cost-benefit ratios of intensive patenting efforts. Universities should develop systems to reliably estimate income from patenting, considering not only internal profits but also external costs, such as the effects on research agendas and the public benefits. Several important questions arise from intensive efforts to generate funds from research developments: (i) Will potential royalty dollars, rather than public need, become an important factor in determining research agendas; (ii) Will public funds be used primarily to support private gain; (iii) Will the perception develop that the wrong people are benefitting from the use of public dollars; (iv) Will public research efforts be driven towards programs that give shorter term results to provide additional support to the institution; and (v) Even if public institutions successfully develop products and techniques with commercial value, will the revenue be large enough to justify the potential risks?

Uncertainty about the Impact of Utility Patents on Plant Research, Particularly Germplasm Enhancement and Crop Development Programs

Some work group members argue that the impact of utility patents will be positive because of greater incentives for research; others fear that the impact will be negative. Public institutions generally have concerns that utility patents will restrict exchange of germplasm and information; on the other hand, industry generally supports utility patents.

It is too early to predict the impact of utility patents on private breeding programs. One central issue is whether or not public plant breeders will maintain a reasonable level of germplasm exchange when they use utility patents. Seed companies have always guarded their materials closely, and have never conducted much germplasm exchange. However, released varieties immediately become germplasm under provisions of the Plant Variety Protection Act (PVPA). This situation may be unaffected, but the effects of utility patents on germplasm exchange and breeding programs should be a focus of the continuing public debate on the impact of IPR changes.

Some work group members suggested that utility patents, particularly on products of public research programs, should have a research exemption component similar to the one available with the PVPA, which allows protected varieties to be used as germplasm. There was concern that broad utility patents on a particular characteristic, which might be widely useful, could seriously impede progress in crop development for the public good. It was suggested that a public debate on the effects of IPR changes and on the effects of utility patents on germplasm exchange and progress in traditional breeding programs be held, perhaps as a USDA forum.

Shifting Paradigm for Agricultural Research

The funds available for traditional research programs are decreasing and institutions are forced to find new sources of support. The use of IPR is only a peripheral issue in the current financial struggles at universities, but it will affect the historical synergisms between public and private researchers. What will be the result of these changing relationships?

Equally important is the potential effect of the use of IPR for income on the university faculty performance and reward system. Will the potential for income from patents drive faculties too strongly toward market concerns? There is concern that some crop programs and research efforts with public significance, but little income potential, will be left behind as the need for income affects research agendas.

Intellectual Property Rights is only one of the many factors affecting research agendas at public institutions. Although material transfer agreements are common, the restrictions that come attached to these agreements complicate research efforts and there is considerable uncertainty about their overall effect on research programs.

Members noted that it is frequently easier to deal with private companies for licensing agreements than universities. Public researchers may have unrealistic income expectations from potential products. That the credibility of public programs will be compromised by income generation efforts must be considered: What would be the effect of a perception of research for profit at a public facility?

University policies regarding the use of patents and germplasm transfer agreements should be made uniform. A model material transfer agreement should be developed.

In the private sector, royalty bearing licensing agreements are commonly used. Strategic alliances have become common and utility patents have contributed to the definition of the roles of the partners in such alliances.

Although some companies have clearly defined patent policies and know what they need to do to protect their developments, there is much uncertainty in other companies—many companies appear to be patenting with a defensive rather than an offensive motivation at the present time. Material transfer agreements generally are highly restrictive; and although they are commonly used, there is concern about the results of these agreements. Intellectual property rights have been the foundation of seed companies, but some types of IPR are now of concern to seed companies. Many companies feel that they need to do more with utility patents, but they are confused about the use of such patents for products of their traditional breeding programs.

Additional Education

We strongly feel there is a need for increased educational and informational efforts about the potential effects of intellectual property rights on public and private research agendas. These should include the following. (i) Concise informational packages on IPR issues for Congress, state legislators, university administrators, public administrators, and industry executives. (Professional societies and the Council for Agricultural Science & Technology should take an important role in this effort.) (ii) Programs to educate Congress and farm organizations about Plant Variety Protection Act of 1970 (PVPA) revisions.

(The USDA, commodity groups and trade associations should be involved in developing these.) There should be a revision of the PVPA to meet the criteria of the 1991 Convention of the International Union for the Protection of New Varieties of Plants (UPOV). (iii) Forums to encourage public debate on the effects of utility patents and IPR; forums to discuss university and federal problems (such as funding problems, pressures for undergraduate teaching, the need for credit for contributions, and so forth). (The USDA is the logical coordinator of these forums.)

CONCLUSIONS

Changes in research agendas of private companies and public institutions resulting from strengthened IPR are inevitable. Seed companies have increased efforts in basic research because of the potential for stronger protection of proprietary developments and fear of loss of competitive position because of utility patents. In general, more private research dollars are being spent on cellular biology, molecular biology, and long-term germplasm enhancement because of the fear of loss of competitive position. The relationship between private industry and universities has changed. Material transfer agreements for access to germplasm from universities are increasingly becoming the norm. Private funding of university research in exchange for an exclusive position has become much more common. The potential for a shift in public research agendas is a serious concern. The perception (or reality) of research for profit could have an adverse effect on public funding of research programs. Educational programs need to be developed that enlighten constituents on the various issues.

Workgroup F: Intellectual Property Rights—Protection of Plant Materials

As a conclusion to the International Workshop on Intellectual Property Rights (IPR), the work group leaders and rapporteurs met to identify the major critical issues identified during the workshop and to propose recommendations for addressing those issues. Using a "brainstorming" process, the participants listed 22 important issues (Table 1). These were explored for commonality, grouped by topics, and ranked for priority. From these, five major issues were identified and recommendations were developed and evaluated for their positive and negative aspects. The results are identified as follows.

ROYALTY INCOME, PARADIGMS, AND SCOPE OF PRIVATELY AND PUBLICLY FUNDED RESEARCH

The work group recommended that an effort be made to inform decision makers about the realities and consequences of seeking institutional income through royalties and licensing, and about the consequences of accepting research funds from private sources, if those funds involve restrictions on access to intellectual property.

The agricultural research community itself should be encouraged to study the consequences of developing and licensing intellectual property at public institutions. The work group also saw a need to counteract the serious erosion of support for agricultural research in the public sector. Concern was voiced about publicly supported institutions seeking alternatives to traditional funding sources during constrained budget times. The pursuit of intellectual property protection could exacerbate the situation.

The participants noted the need for cooperation between the public and private sectors in developing intellectual property, while improving the ability of public institutions to manage their intellectual property.

It was suggested that the reports of this workshop could contribute greatly in providing information to decision makers and communicating some of the consequences of the increasingly constrained funding for public sector agricultural research. Public researchers will have increased pressure to seek outside funds, which will require public institutions to establish policies for protecting intellectual property. The initiation of licensing or other agreements with research sponsors may affect the direction of research, including shifts in research priorities and redirection based on marginal funds.

Table 1. Critical issues† related to intellectual property rights and protection of plant materials.

1.	Generation of research income for universities
2.	Education of the players
3.	Shifting paradigm of agricultural research
4.	Management of intellectual property rights, consistent with licensing practices
5.	Public-private communications
6.	Need/lack of research exemptions
7.	International dimensions of intellectual property rights
8.	Identification of all players in intellectual property rights
9.	Distinction of intellectual property from intellectual property rights
10.	Effective licensing by universities on public acceptance and public trust/mistrust
11.	Farmer exemptions
12.	Affects of intellectual property rights on germplasm exchange
13.	Role and scope of privately and publicly funded research
14.	Broad social impact of intellectual property rights
15.	Modification of the Plant Variety Protection Act re: UPOV-1991
16.	Enforcement of intellectual property rights
17.	Impact on major/minor species
18.	Compensation of third world for germplasm
19.	Accommodation of plant breeders and biotechnology
20.	Effect of utility patents on plant breeding
21.	Access to protected and unprotected materials
22.	Royalties to public plant breeders and the consequences

† The following combinations of the above items comprised the topics of the work groups: A = 1 + 3 + 13, B = 2 + 8 + 5 + 9, C = 20 + 21 + 12, D = 7 + 18, E = 10 + 14, and F = 11 + 15 + 16.

EDUCATION AND COMMUNICATION

The work group recommended that the results of this workshop be used by professional societies to disseminate information about IPR. Opportunities should be developed and mechanisms found, for providing better communications across the agricultural research sectors, perhaps through journals and other forms of communication.

Another recommendation was to reassess society's role in and support of public sector agricultural research. Concomitant with this, the participants noted the need to increase society's scientific literacy and to demonstrate the importance of science as a part of agriculture. A reassessment could be done by convening related groups to obtain information and a broad perspective on intellectual property via, for example, plant germplasm.

Another recommendation was to develop model license agreements that include points to consider when establishing agreements concerning IPR. Pubic institutions should seek help with the management of intellectual property rights. This could include the study of other countries and scientific fields for models that might apply to issues of plant germplasm access and intellectual property protection.

A forum should also be established to conduct dialogue with industrial executives on the needs of academic institutions regarding intellectual property management. Public institutions should assemble available information regarding intellectual property management and encourage the targeted distribution of that information within the public agricultural research system.

The work group noted that efforts aimed at these problems will be ongoing.

FARMER EXEMPTIONS, UPOV, AND ENFORCEMENT OF PROTECTION

In 1991, modifications were made to the International Union for the Protection of New Varieties of Plants (UPOV) agreements that now should be incorporated into the U.S. Plant Variety Protection Act of 1970 (PVPA). The work group recommended that the USDA assume the lead role in making these necessary modifications to improve the attractiveness of plant variety protection through utility patents, and at the same time, provide better products with a clearer understanding of the options for their marketing without infringement on property rights.

Changes to PVPA should include an assessment of how best to provide compliance and enforcement. Presently, intellectual property owners are responsible for enforcement, but an evaluation is needed to determine whether state and federal agencies should also be responsible for enforcement. Currently, some states regulate aspects of the PVPA (e.g., by labels).

The participants noted that there may be some difficulties in implementing the 1991 UPOV provisions. For instance, the concept and definition of ''essentially derived varieties'' is not sufficiently clear. The implementation of provisions for ''farmer exemptions'' may be legally complicated, in that this is not in the 1991 UPOV Convention, but hinges on a country to provide. Thus, U.S. language must be clearly written. It was further recommended that when implementing these changes, the USDA should ask for broad input from affected groups.

PATENTS, AND GERMPLASM ACCESS AND EXCHANGE

The work group recommended that research exemptions be provided with utility patents on plants. This would allow greater availability of germplasm and lessen the fear of reduced accessibility that now seems to be prevalent in the academic research community. Licensing intellectual property can provide greater access and enhance international exchange, but the academic community is hesitant to endorse a system that could become clerically cumbersome.

The work group recommended that all deposits of plant genetic materials become part of the national germplasm system. This recommendation is especially pertinent for materials covered by PVPA, which are presently not accessible. Plant genetic materials in the national plant germplasm system are distributed freely to scientists worldwide.

Another recommendation of the work group was to encourage public institutions (e.g., land grant universities, Agricultural Research Service) to give research exemptions through licenses. The participants saw a need to encourage public discussion and debate on the merits of utility patent protection with plants. Such discussions should explore the consequences of broad patent claims in the absence of a legislatively provided research exemption for utility patents.

However, a consideration of these recommendations is that if utility patent research exemptions are implemented, private companies may be inclined to safeguard their intellectual property with trade secrets rather than utility patents of plant materials. This could limit the availability of plant germplasm within the broad scientific community.

INTERNATIONAL DIMENSIONS AND COMPENSATION

The participants recommended the use of plant breeders' rights in developing countries as a means of enhancing the development and the exchange of plant germplasm. It was further recommended that country-to-country plant germplasm exchanges be facilitated by whatever means appropriate. It was felt that discussions should be encouraged and actions taken to address the equity issues in germplasm exchanges, which include compensation to countries of origin.

CONCLUSIONS

These recommendations are intended to increase access to world plant genetic resources and to enhance the public and private sectors' activities in developing new cultivars. It was acknowledged by the working group that accomplishing these objectives would be difficult, but they are certainly worthy of attention.

Appendix 1: Pertinent Available Publications

International Convention for the Protection of New Varieties of Plants of December 2, 1961, as revised at Geneva on November 10, 1972, on October 23, 1978, and on March 19, 1991. 1991. International Union for the Protection of New Varieties of Plants, Geneva.

United States Department of Agriculture—Agricultural Marketing Service. 1989. United States Plant Variety Protection Act of December 24, 1970 (84 Stat. 1542, 7 U.S.C. 2321 et seq.). U.S. Gov. Print. Office, Washington, DC.

Appendix 2. ESSENTIALLY DERIVED VARIETIES Document prepared by the Office of the International Union for the Protection of New Varieties of Plants Geneva, Switzerland

I. Introduction

1. The 1991 Act of the International Convention for the Protection of New Varieties of Plants ("the 1991 Act") contains in Article 14(5) provisions which extend the scope of protection afforded to the breeder of a protected variety under the provisions of Article 14(1) to (4) to "varieties which are essentially derived from the protected variety, where the protected variety is not itself an essentially derived variety."

2. The Diplomatic Conference for the Revision of the International Conventionfor the Protection of New Varieties of Plants (UPOV) held in Geneva from March 4 to 19, 1991, which unanimously adopted the text of the 1991 Act, resolved (see document DC/91/140) "to request the Secretary-General of UPOV to start work immediately after the Conference on the establishment of draft standard guidelines, for adoption by the Council of UPOV, on essentially derived varieties."

3. Discussion in the Diplomatic Conference prior to the adoption of the above-mentioned resolution suggested:

(a) that any guidelines adopted should have no legally binding force;

(b) that any guidelines adopted could not or should not change the essence of the provisions of the Convention or its interpretation;

(c) that the provisions concerning essential derivation were an integral part of provisions establishing the scope of the breeder's protection; that it was the responsibility of the breeder to establish and defend the scope of protection of his variety in relation to that of other varieties; that guide- lines addressed to the Governments of member States might therefore be inappropriate.

II. Nature of Guidelines

4. With the endorsement of its Council, UPOV publishes:

(i) Guidelines for the conduct of tests for distinctness, homogeneity and stability of new varieties of plants for individual species;

(ii) a General Introduction to such guidelines which gives guidance to member States upon the general principles involved in the conduct of tests for distinctness, homogeneity and stability;

(iii) UPOV Recommendations on Variety Denominations.

Such guidelines and recommendations relate in each case to conditions or requirements which must be satisfied prior to a grant of protection for a variety. Since the granting of protection is a matter for the competent authorities of member States, such guidelines and recommendations are, in effect, guidelines and recommendations in relation to the practice of the Offices of member States and addressed to the Governments of member States.

5. Article 5 of the 1991 Act specifies the conditions for the grant of a breeder's right and provides that the grant of a breeder's right shall not be subject to ''any further or different conditions.'' Matters relating to essential derivation are not included in the criteria to be satisfied prior to the grant of a breeder's right. A purported finding of ''essential derivation'' by a national office at the time of grant might constitute the imposition of a ''further condition'' or a qualification attaching to the grant and as such be contrary to the provisions of the 1991 Act. This conclusion is consistent with the view repeatedly expressed by delegates in the Diplomatic Conference and in preparatory meetings for the Diplomatic Conference that the existence of a relationship of essential derivation between two protected varieties is a matter for the holders of rights in the varieties. This being so, any guidelines concerning the nature of essential derivation will necessarily be of a fundamentally different nature to existing UPOV guidelines and recommendations which are addressed to member States and concern the practice of their Offices.

III. The Provisions of the 1991 Act Concerning Essential Derivation

6. The full text of Article 14(5) of the 1991 Act reads as follows:

''(5) [Essentially derived and certain other varieties] (a) The provisions of paragraphs (1) to (4) shall also apply in relation to
(i) varieties which are essentially derived from the protected variety, where the protected variety is not itself an essentially derived variety,
(ii) varieties which are not clearly distinguishable in accordance with Article 7 from the protected variety and
(iii) varieties whose production requires the repeated use of the protected variety.

(b) For the purposes of sub-paragraph (a)(i), a variety shall be deemed to be essentially derived from another variety (''the initial variety'') when
(i) it is predominantly derived from the initial variety, or from a variety that is itself predominantly derived from the initial variety, while

retaining the expression of the essential characteristics that result from the genotype or combination of genotypes of the initial variety,
(ii) it is clearly distinguishable from the initial variety and
(iii) except for the differences which result from the act of derivation, it conforms to the initial variety in the expression of the essential characteristics that result from the genotype or combination of genotypes of the initial variety.

(c) Essentially derived varieties may be obtained for example by the selection of a natural or induced mutant, or of a somaclonal variant, the selection of a variant individual from plants of the initial variety, backcrossing, or transformation by genetic engineering.''

The specific wording used in the above provisions is examined in the paragraphs which follow.

7. ''where the protected variety is not itself an essentially derived variety'' (Article 14(5)(a)(i)): The underlined words relate to a situation where, for example, Variety C is essentially derived from Variety B which is in turn essentially derived from Variety A. The words make clear that Variety C does not fall within the scope of the protection of Variety B; the words are not intended and should not be interpreted to require the rights' holder to positively prove that the protected variety is not itself an essentially derived variety before he is able to exercise the rights conferred by Article 14(5)(a)(i). The words provide an opportunity for the breeder of an alleged ''essentially derived variety'' to show that the initial variety is itself an essentially derived variety.

8. ''predominantly derived from the initial variety'' (Article 14(5)(b)(i): The requirement of predominant derivation from an initial variety means that a variety can only be essentially derived from one variety. Discussions of the revision proposals in the sessions of the Administrative and Legal Committee which preceded the adoption by the Council in October 1990 of a draft Convention consistently showed that the intention was that a variety should only be essentially derived from another variety when it retained virtually the whole genotype of the other variety. This is confined by the words commented upon in paragraph 9 below. A derived variety could not in practice retain the expression of the essential characteristics of the variety from which it is derived unless it is almost entirely derived from that variety.

9. ''while retaining the expression of the essential characteristics'': The essential characteristics are those which are indispensable or fundamental to the variety. ''Characteristics'' would seem to embrace all features of a variety including, for example, morphological, physiological, agronomic, industrial and biochemical characteristics. It is suggested that the result of a biochemical test conducted on a variety, for instance, a screening test using a genetic probe, is

a characteristic of the variety. ''while retaining'' requires that the expression of the essential characteristics be derived from the initial variety.

10. ''that result from the genotype'': These words make clear that only characteristics of a variety which are heritable genetically should be taken into account. Any descriptive features of plant material that represent environmental effects should be disregarded. It has been questioned whether the test result arising from the use of a genetic probe, e.g. an RFLP, is a characteristic that ''results from the genotype.'' It has been suggested that the test result of using such a probe ''results from the genotype.''

11. ''(ii) it is clearly distinguishable from the initial variety'': These words establish that essential derivation is concerned only with varieties that are clearly distinguishable from an initial variety and which are accordingly protectable independently from the initial variety.

12. ''(iii) except for the differences which result from the act of derivation it conforms to the initial variety in the expression of the essential characteristics that result from the genotype or combination of genotypes of the original variety'': The words ''except for the differences which result from the act of derivation'' do not set a limit to the amount of difference which may exist where a variety is considered to be essentially derived. A limit is, however, set by the words of subparagraph (i). The differences must not be such that the variety fails ''to retain the expression of the essential characteristics that result from the genotype or combination of genotypes of the initial variety.'' A comparison between subparagraphs (i) and (iii) of Article 14(5)(b) is somewhat problematic in that (i) would seem to require the whole of the expression of the essential characteristics that result from the genotype of the initial variety while (iii) requires only that the derived variety conform to the initial variety except for differences resulting from the act of derivation (however, see the discussions in paragraph 13 below). The examples of essential derivation given in Article 14(5)(c) make clear that the differences which result from the act of derivation should be one or very few.

IV. Establishing the ''essential derivation'' of a Variety.

13. Article 14(5)(b) lays down those conditions that must be satisfied in order that a later variety shall be deemed to be essentially derived from another variety (''the initial variety''). The second of those conditions (established in Article 14(5)(b)(ii)) requires only that the later variety be clearly distinguishable from the initial variety and requires no further comment. The first such condition (established in Article 14(5)(b)(i)) requires that the later variety be derived from the initial variety which in turn requires that genetic materials of the initial variety have been used in the creation of the later variety. The first condition is accordingly concerned with the genetic origin of the later variety. The third such condition (established in Article 14(5)(b)(iii)) requires that the

later variety conforms to ("is made similar to") the initial variety in the expression of the inherited essential characteristics of the initial variety apart from the differences which result from the act of derivation. The third condition is accordingly concerned with the degree of similarity of the later variety to the initial variety. Whilst the first condition also makes reference to the degree of similarity, the primary function of the first condition is to establish a requirement relating to the genetic origin of the variety.

14. The question of the genetic origin of the later variety posed by Article 14(5)(b)(i) is primarily a question of fact to be established using all available evidence including the personal testimony of individual witnesses, laboratory and field record books, knowledge concerning the inheritance of particular characteristics, the results of biochemical tests and so on. The question of the degree of similarity of the later variety to the initial variety primarily calls for a value judgement whether the later variety does or does not conform to the initial variety in the expression of its essential, heritable characteristics.

V. The Question of the Genetic Origin

15. A major difficulty in practice in the implementation of legal provisions relating to essential derivation for litigants alleging infringement will be establishing as a matter of fact that Variety A is derived from Variety B, where this fact is not admitted by the defendant in the action or has not been otherwise admitted in a public document. Derivation will be inferred in many cases from the weight of evidence concerning the variety's genetic origins (how could such a degree of similarity have resulted unless A were derived from B?) but difficulty will remain in some cases.

16. Some help could be provided by national offices if they were to demand more precise and meaningful information on genealogy in technical questionnaires addressed to applicants for protection and if the completed questionnaires could be made available for search in all member States by parties able to demonstrate a bona fide interest. It should not be acceptable, for example, that all information relating to genealogy is presented in the form of meaningless codes.

17. Another possibility raised by an international non-governmental organization, but not taken up by UPOV in the revision process, would be to provide in national laws for some modification of the burden of proof. The suggestion, modified so as to relate to the text of Article 14(5), was that once the plaintiff in an infringement action establishes that an alleged essentially derived variety expresses the essential characteristics that result from the genotype or combination of genotypes of the initial variety, the burden of proof should fall upon the defendant to establish that his variety was not derived from the initial variety. In view of the precise records kept by serious

plant breeders, the defendant would be in a uniquely strong position to provide evidence on this point.

18. Whilst it is normally the responsibility of the plaintiff in an infringement action to establish the fact of infringement, the UPOV Convention is silent upon the question of the burden of proof and it is open to member States to modify the normal burden of proof should they wish to do so. It should be noted that a similar proposal to reverse the burden of proof is contained in Article 24 of the "Basic Proposal for the Treaty and Regulation" submitted to the Diplomatic Conference for the Conclusion of a Treaty supplementing the Paris Convention as far as Patents are concerned, the first part of which was held in The Hague, Netherlands, in June 1991. The proposal of the said Article 24 concerns the reversal of the burden of proof in infringement proceedings concerning processes for obtaining products where the plaintiff has in many cases a difficult or impossible task to prove use of the process while the defendant can with ease demonstrate that he did not use the process.

VI. The Question of the Degree of Similarity

19. A judgement on the question of the degree of similarity must be reached on the basis of the essential characteristics which result from the genotype. "Essential" has the meanings "fundamental" or "indispensable." The language finally adopted in Article 14(5)(iii) replaced Article 14(2)(b)(iii) in the Basic Proposal considered by the Diplomatic Conference. Article 14(2)(b)(iii) of the Basic Proposal provided that the essentially derived variety must "conform to the genotype or combination of genotypes of the initial variety ..." This language was initially replaced by the adoption by the Conference of the proposal of Japan contained in document DC/91/66 which proposed that Article 14(2)(b)(iii) of the Basic Proposal be reworded to read:

> "(iii) the characteristics that are the expression of its genotype or its combination of genotypes conform to those of the initial variety apart from the differences which result from the method of derivation."

It is suggested that Article 14(2)(b)(iii) of the Basic Proposal and the Japanese proposal which replaced it called for the degree of similarity between varieties to be assessed on the basis of the characteristics of the variety taken as a whole and not on the basis of individual characteristics taken in isolation. The language of the Japanese proposal was subsequently amended by the Drafting Committee but it is suggested that no change in substance was intended. It is suggested that it should not be possible to conclude that a derived variety does not attain the necessary degree of similarity simply because it does not express one single characteristic (perhaps very simply inherited) taken in isolation.

20. Taken individually the characteristics that are "essential" would vary from species to species, from variety to variety, and even from member State to member State. It is clearly not desirable that decisions on whether a variety

is or is not essentially derived should be taken differently in UPOV member States.

21. To fulfill the conditions imposed by Article 14(5)(b)(iii) a later variety must conform to the initial variety in the expression of the essential heritable characteristics of the initial variety "except for the differences which result from the act of derivation". Theoretically, if variety A is crossed with variety B and variety X is selected from the resulting progeny, if variety X derives less than half of its essential heritable characteristics (i.e. of its genotype) from A and more than half from B, it will be essentially derived from B since apart from the characteristics derived from A, it conforms to the expression of the essential characteristics of B. This is clearly not the intended interpretation. A later variety cannot fulfill the conditions of Article 14(5)(b)(i) unless it is predominantly derived from the initial variety while retaining, without qualification in Article 14(5)(b)(i), the expression of the essential heritable characteristics of the initial variety.

22. Examples of possible essential derivation are set out, as a basis for discussion, in the annex to this document.

ANNEX

Example 1: A pyramid

[Each $^{+}$ is a characteristic added by genetic engineering or complete back-crossing and controlled by a single gene or by a few closely linked genes]

Variety A - the initial protected variety

Variety A^{+} - is distinct from and predominantly derived from A

Variety A^{++} - is distinct from A^{+} and is predominantly derived from A^{+}

Variety A^{+++} - is distinct from A^{++} and is predominantly derived from A^{++}.

1.1 Question: Is variety A^{+} essentially derived from A?

1.1 Answer:

Yes, if it is predominantly derived in such a way that it retains the expression of the essential inherited characteristics (that is the characteristics that "result from the genotype") of the initial variety AND if in the final result, except for the differences which result from the act of derivation (added characteristic^{+} in this case) it conforms as required by Article 14(5)(b)(iii).

1.2 Question: Is variety A^{++} essentially derived from A^{+}?

1.2 Answer:

(i) Same answer as for 1.1. but with different consequences. Since variety A^{+} is itself essentially derived from A, it fails to satisfy the requirement of Article 14(5)(a)(i). Accordingly the scope of protection of variety A^{+} does not cover variety A^{++}.

(ii) Variety A^{++} may, however, be essentially derived from variety A if it retains the expression of the essential inherited characteristics of variety A and if it conforms as required by Article 14(5)(b)(iii).

1.3 Question: Is variety A^{+++} essentially derived from variety A and if so how many further characteristics can be added to it before it ceases to be essentially derived from A?

1.3 Answer:

Variety A^{+++} will be essentially derived from A if it satisfies the provision of Article 14(5)(b)(i) and (iii). Varieties with further added characteristics similarly derived would continue to be essentially derived until such time as a variety is developed which ceases to conform to the initial variety in the expressions of its essential characteristics inherited from A. A decision on this question in an infringement suit would be a value judgement based upon the available evidence.

Example 2: Reselection

2.1 A protected variety of a self-pollinating species has two elements A and B which were not separately identified and described at the date of the grant of protection. A breeder selects component B from the variety and seeks to protect it as a new variety.

2.1 Question: Will the new variety be essentially derived from the protected variety? Does the position vary if:

(a) the protected variety comprised 50% element A and 50% B
(b) the protected variety comprised 80% element A and 20% B
(c) the protected variety comprised 95% element A and 5% B
(d) the protected variety comprised 99.9% element A and 0.1% B

Is the position different if B is very different genetically from A?

2.1 Answer:

(i) A supplementary question to ask prior to giving an answer would seem to be: "Is element B part of the variety?" The answer to this question may vary depending upon the law and practice of individual member States. In all countries where the identity of the variety is established by the definitive sample of propagating material of the variety rather than a written description, element B will be part of the variety if it is present in the definitive sample and if it is appropriately related genetically to element A.

(ii) Where element B is not appropriately related genetically to element A (for example, it is an outcrossing or a physical admixture and does not result from residual genetic variation) and it is present at less than the 5% level, it could be argued that element B is not part of the variety particularly where it has not been identified and described at the date of grant of protection.

(iii) Where element B is part of the variety (that is it represents residual genetic variation) and present in excess of 0.1% of the variety, a selection of element B might not be considered to be a distinct variety. The selection of element B, present at the 0.1% level or less, if considered to be part of the variety (that is it represents residual genetic variation and is not an admixture or an outcrossing) would be derived from the protected variety.

(iv) Whether element B would or would not be an essentially derived variety would depend upon whether it satisfied the requirements of Article 14(5)(b)(iii).

2.2 A breeder selects on the basis of earliness one hundred clones from a population of plants of a protected cross-pollinating forage variety A. A new variety B results from the cross-pollination of the selected clones and is distinct from the protected variety A on the basis of earliness.

2.2 Question: Is the new variety B essentially derived from the protected variety A? Would the position change if only 5 clones were selected?

2.2 Answer:

(i) The example tells one that the new variety B is clearly distinguishable from the initial variety on the basis of earliness. It is clearly "predominantly derived" from the initial variety A by selection in the sense that all the initial variation comes from variety A. Additionally a judgment must be made whether the new variety B has been so derived that it retains the expression of the essential characteristics which result from the combination of genotypes of the initial variety A. This will depend in the first instance on the number of clones selected and whether the clones are a representative sample of the original combination of genotypes (apart from earliness). Finally a value judgment must be made on the extent of similarity between variety A and variety B to satisfy Article 14(5)(b)(iii).

(ii) In principle, it would seem more likely that the expression of the essential characteristics of variety A would be retained and that variety B "conforms" with variety A where the new variety B is based upon 100 clones than where it is based on five.

(iii) One may speculate that the greater the number of genes controlling the introduced characteristic (earliness in this example), the more likely it would be that the expression of other essential characteristics would also change so that variety B would no longer retain the expression of the essential characteristics of variety A or conform so as to satisfy Article 14(5)(b)(iii).

2.3 A breeder plants in a greenhouse many thousands of seeds of a protected alfalfa variety A, 0.1% of whose plants are resistant to a disease. The breeder inoculates the resulting seedlings with the disease and selects the survivors, which are grown on, flower, cross-pollinate and set seed. The seed produces plants which are screened and selected as before. The cycle is repeated a number of times until the percentage of resistant plants in the population is increased to 40%. The selection scheme is designed to ensure that the gene frequencies of the protected variety are as far as possible maintained with the exception of the gene responsible for resistance whose frequency is increased. 200 resistant plants are cloned and allowed to cross-pollinate to produce breeders seed of a new resistant variety B.

2.3 Question: Is the new variety B essentially derived from the protected variety A?

2.3 Answer:

(i) The new variety B is clearly distinguishable from and is predominantly derived from the initial variety A.

(ii) If variety B retains and conforms to the expression of the essential characteristics that result from the combination of genotypes of variety A (apart from the introduced disease resistance) it will be essentially derived. It is suggested that statistical approaches similar to those used for distinctness testing would be necessary to demonstrate that variety B did so retain and conform to the expression of the essential characteristics of variety A. If the disease resistance is governed by a single resistant gene, it is more likely that the expression of the essential characteristics that result from the combination of genotypes of variety B will be retained and conform so as to satisfy Article 14(5)(b)(iii).

Example 3: Backcrossing

3.1 Simply inherited characteristics

Variety B is used as the recurrent parent which is backcrossed eight times on to variety A. The object of the program is to transfer to variety B a disease resistance characteristic governed by a single gene of variety A; the resulting disease resistant variety B^+ is clearly distinguishable from B.

3.1 Question: Is the new variety B^+ essentially derived from B?

3.1 Answer:

Since variety B^+ seems likely to have retained the essential characteristics that result from the genotype of variety B and to conform so as to satisfy Article 14(5)(b)(iii) (apart from the added disease resistance) it will be essentially derived.

3.2 Characteristics of complex inheritance

The same facts as in example 3.1, except that the disease resistance characteristic, say soybean cyst nematode resistance, is governed by several genes and the screening is technically complex and involves difficult and expensive trials for the screening of each backcross generation.

3.2 Question: Is the resulting soybean cyst nematode resistant variety B^+ essentially derived from B? Does the position vary as the number of backcross generations is reduced and the breeder selects in the segregating progeny? At what point would B^+ cease to be essentially derived from B?

3.2 Answer:

(i) The amount of effort or expenses involved in the development of the soybean cyst nematode resistant variety is irrelevant.

(ii) The fact that the inheritance of the resistance factor is complex will be relevant only insofar as the variety is not derived so as to retain the essential characteristics that result from the genotype of the initial variety and does not conform so as to satisfy Article 14(5)(b)(iii).

(iii) The number of backcross generations is relevant only to the extent that it throws light on whether the variety is likely to be derived while retaining the essential characteristics that result from the genotype of the initial variety.

Example 4: Transformation by genetic engineering

Variety A is transformed by genetic engineering so as to incorporate and express a desirable gene. 100 plants are successfully transformed and screened to select a plant which retains the maximum number of the characteristics of A with the optimal expression of the desirable gene. The selected plant is used as the basis of variety A^+.

4.1 Question: Is variety A^+ essentially derived from variety A? Does the position change if

(a) it is necessary to modify and select within many thousands of plants to identify the desirable plant, or

(b) it was expensive and difficult to develop the transformation process?

4.1 Answer:

(i) Variety A^+ is likely to be clearly distinguishable from variety A on the basis of the expression of the desirable $gene^+$ and is clearly predominantly derived from variety A.

(ii) The effort, experience and difficulty of incorporating $gene^+$ into variety A is irrelevant, as such, but may throw light on the extent to which the derived variety retains the expression of the essential characteristics that result from the genotype of variety A.

(iii) Whether variety A^+ is essentially derived will depend upon whether it has (apart from the difference resulting from $gene^+$) retained the expression of the essential characteristics that result from the genotype of variety A and conforms so as to satisfy Article 14(5)(b)(iii). It can be expected that in many cases variety A^+ will be essentially derived from variety A.

Example 5: Somaclonal variants

Cells derived from variety A are maintained in tissue culture in the form of callus. Plants are regenerated from such callus tissue and include variants from variety A which are distinct and stable.

5.1 Question: Are such variants essentially derived from variety A? Does the position change if the genetic differences between such variants are small or large?

5.1 Answer:

(i) The variants will be predominantly derived from variety A.

(ii) Whether a variety based upon a particular variant will be essentially derived will depend upon whether it retains the essential characteristics resulting from the genotype of variety A and apart from specified differences resulting from selection it conforms so as to satisfy Article 14(5)(b)(iii).

(iii) If the selected difference is very large it will be less likely that the variant will so retain such essential characteristics. A variety based on such a variant will thus be less likely to be essentially derived from variety A.

Example 6: Natural and induced mutations

A mutation is discovered in variety A and used to create a new variety B.

6.1 Question: Is variety B essentially derived from variety A? Does the position differ if the mutation results from a simple genetic change or if the change is more complex, or if the mutation is artificially induced?

Answer:

(i) Variety B is predominantly derived from variety A and is clearly distinguishable from variety A.

(ii) Whether the mutation is naturally or artificially induced is irrelevant.

(iii) The only remaining questions are whether variety B is derived from variety A while retaining the expression of the essential characteristics that result from the genotype of variety A and whether variety B conforms with variety A so as to satisfy Article 14(5)(b)(iii). In most cases this will be so and variety B will be essentially derived from variety A.

(iv) The complexity of the genetic change may, however, result in a mutation that no longer retains the expression of the essential characteristics that result from the genotype of variety A. In this case variety B would not be essentially derived from variety A.

(v) Where variety A is a mutation of an unprotected variety X, variety B may be essentially derived from variety A but will not fall within the scope of protection of variety A since variety A is itself an essentially derived variety. This fact will be of importance for species where mutation breeding is a frequently used technique.

Example 7: Change of chromosome number

The opinions differ on whether varieties resulting from the doubling or halving of the chromosome number should or should not be regarded as retaining the expression of the essential characteristics that result from the genotype or combination of genotypes of the initial variety. It is suggested that the criteria of essential derivation can be applied where the breeding technique involves a change in chromosome number in exactly the same way as with other breeding techniques.

Example 8: Cell fusion

A breeder transfers the nucleus from a cell of variety A into a cell from variety B with differing and alien cytoplasm, in which the nucleus of variety B has been destroyed, with a view to creating a male sterile version of variety A.

8.1 Question: Will the male sterile line be essentially derived?

8.1 Answer:

(i) The male sterile version of variety A will be clearly distinguishable from variety A on the basis of its male sterility and will be predominantly derived genetically from variety A (it is suggested that the small amount of DNA derived from the cytoplasmic organelles of variety B would be irrelevant) so as to retain the essential characteristics that result from the genotype of variety A.

(ii) It will be a question of judgment whether the male sterile version of variety A conforms to the expression of the heritable characteristics of variety A apart from the introduced male sterility so as to satisfy Article 14(5)(b)(iii).

Appendix 3. Program

26–28 January 1993
Holiday Inn–Capitol
550 C Street, SW
Washington, DC 20024
Phone: (202) 479-4000

Sponsors

Crop Science Society of America
American Society for Horticultural Science
American Society of Agronomy
Soil Science Society of America
U.S. Department of Agriculture-Science and Education

Tuesday, 26 January

Columbia Room

6:00 pm **Registration**

Presiding: Richard Lower, University of Wisconsin, Madison, WI

7:00 **Workshop Overview:**

Victor Lechtenberg, *Purdue University, W. Lafayette, IN*

Goals and expectations will be explained to set the stage for the workshop.

7:10 **Introduction: Intellectual Property Rights Workshop**

John Barton, *Stanford Law School, Stanford, CA*

7:40 **Goals of Inventors, Owners, and Users**

Donald N. Duvick, *Iowa State University, Ames, IA*
Richard Lower, *University of Wisconsin, Madison, WI*
Dean Plowman, *USDA-ARS, Washington, DC*

These presentations will provide an orientation of the goals and expectations associated with intellectual property rights as related to the structure of the industry, university, and governmental sectors of the intellectual property community.

8:25 **Implications for US Inventors on Non-US Protection Procedures and Practices**

Barry Greengrass, *International Union for the Protection of New Varieties of Plants, Geneva, Switzerland*

The focus of this presentation will be on providing a background for US inventors and administrators on procedures and practices for intellectual property in other countries. How can the differences in protecting plant materials be resolved?

9:00 **Reception (Clark Room)**

10:00 **Recess**

Wednesday, 27 January

Columbia Room

Presiding: Charles W. Stuber, USDA-ARS, Raleigh, NC

8:00 am **Status of IPR Protection**

Nicholas J. Seay, *Quarles & Brady, Madison, WI*

Elizabeth C. Weimar, *U.S. Patent and Trademark Office, Department of Commerce, Washington, DC*

Alan Atchley, *Plant Variety Protection Office, USDA, Beltsville, MD*

An oversight perspective of all forms of intellectual property rights as applied to the protection of plant materials will be presented. Specific updates on the status of activities in the Patent Trademark Office and the Plant Variety Protection Office will be provided.

9:00 **Science Based Identification of Plant Genetic Materials**

Bruce Hunter, *CIBA-GEIGY, Greensboro, NC*

Provide an overview of science based identification of plant genetic materials and the implications for enforcing property rights. Identify the potential role of scientific evidence to differentiate among varieties and the legal interpretation for enforcement of property rights.

9:30 **National Legislative Issues**

Terry L. Nipp, AESOP Enterprises, Ltd., Washington, DC

Presentation will provide an update on pending legislative or administrative proposals that affect intellectual property rights.

10:00 **Break (Columbia Foyer)**

Presiding: Thomas A. Fretz, Iowa State University, Ames, IA

10:20 **Case History Examples**

This session will review several real world examples that represent the most contentious issues. These issues will then be addressed in the break-out sessions. Resource people will be invited to present brief vignettes of no more than 10 minutes from different perspectives for each topic. Those presenting the vignettes are asked to prepare a brief summary statement of one page to be handed out to all participants.

A. Licensing of Protected Property.

Eldon E. Ortman, *Purdue University, W. Lafayette, IN*

Examples of exclusive and non-exclusive licensing will be presented, including opportunities for cross licensing

B. Exemptions.

David Houser, *Wisconsin Alumni Research Foundation, Madison, WI*

Research exemption in patent law—how it works in practice. Farmers exemption and its effectiveness for plant variety protection. The use of license language to achieve exemptions for research and other purposes will be reviewed.

C. Exchanges.

Henry L. Shands, *USDA-ARS, Beltsville, MD*

Dennis Hoerner, Jr., *Monsanto, St. Louis, MO*

Impact of IPR on exchange among domestic and foreign scientists of whole plant living materials and molecular genetic processes/biotechnology tools such as genetic/genome maps, clones, and probes.

D. Ethical and Social Issues of Protection.

Larry M. Busch, *Michigan State University, E. Lansing, MI*

How they have been addressed or ignored from a private and public perspective.

E. Research Agendas.

Keith A. Walker, *Agrigenetics Co., Eastlake, OH*

Charles Hess, *University of California, Davis, CA*

The presenters will discuss the impacts of intellectual property protection on the private and public agendas.

F. Synthesis and Recommendations Including Policy and Legal Considerations.

Fred Bliss, *University of California, Davis, CA*

Representatives will be identified from each of the Break-Out Work Groups (A through E) to assist in synthesizing a consensus of recommendations, including policy and legal considerations, and for implementation through post meeting activities. Individuals assigned to this Work Group will meet with the individual Break-Out Work Groups A–E during the afternoon. After the Break-Out Work Group reports are presented in the Wednesday evening general session, members of Work Group F will convene as a separate body to synthesize a consensus of recommendations and a proposed plan for their implementation.
(The first formal meeting of the Work Group will be on Thursday morning at 8:00 am in the Mercury Room.)

1:20 **Break-Out Work Groups Convene**

Introduction of Chairs and Rapporteurs for each work group and review of the charge and scheduling for the break-out sessions. NOTE: Workshop office located in Suite 943.

A. Licensing: Saturn

Chair: Neal DeVos, *Elkhorn Res. & Dev. Co., Castroville, CA*

Rapporteur: Robert Jondle, *Henderson & Sturm, Omaha, NE*

B. Exemptions: Venus

Chair: Mike Roth, *Pioneer Hi-Bred International, Des Moines, IA*

Rapporteur: William Tallent, *USDA-ARS, Washington, DC*

C. Exchanges: Jupiter

Chair: Calvin Qualset, *University of California-Davis*

Rapporteur: Ronald Cantrell, *Iowa State University, Ames*

D. Ethical and Social Issues of Protection: Columbia A/Apollo

Chair: Gary Heichel, *University of Illinois, Urbana*

Rapporteur: Edward Ryder, *USDA-ARS, Salinas, CA*

E. Research Agendas: Columbia B/Gemini

Chair: James R. Fischer, *Clemson University, Clemson, SC*

Rapporteur: Allen Stevens, *Petoseed Co., Woodland, CA*

F. Synthesis and Recommendations: Mars

Chair: Fred Bliss, *University of California, Davis, CA*

Vice Chairs:

David R. MacKenzie, *USDA-CSRS, Washington, DC*
Jody Giesser, *Amoco Corp., Naperville, IL*

3:00 **Break (Columbia Foyer)**

3:20 **Break-Out Groups Reconvene**

5:30 **Break**

6:00 **Reception (Clark Room Foyer)**

7:00 **Dinner (Clark Room)**

8:15 **Break-Out Work Group Reports to be presented in General Session (Columbia Room)**

Brief five minute reports from each Break-Out Work Group will be presented to aid in focusing each work group's activities and to alleviate undue duplication.

Thursday, 28 January

8:00 **Break-Out Work Groups Reconvene**

Review discussion and interaction with other work groups and prepare for the final report.

Break-Out Work Group F will convene in the Mercury Room, which will be the first formal meeting of this Work Group.

9:30 **Break (Columbia Foyer)**

Presiding: Thomas A. Fretz, Iowa State University, Ames, IA

9:50 **General Session (Columbia Room)**

Final reports will be presented by a representative of each Break-Out Work Group. Discussion will be allowed to the extent possible.

12:30 **Lunch (Clark Room)**

1:30 **Adjourn**

(Work Group Chairs and Rapporteurs are to meet with members of the Steering Committee and the Synthesis and Recommendations Work Group to finalize the Work Group Reports and the initial draft of the Proceedings.)

Steering Committee

Co-chairs:
Victor L. Lechtenberg and Richard L. Lower

Members
Steve Baenziger
Robert F Barnes
Howard J. Brooks
Donald N. Duvick, ex officio
Kenneth H. Evans
Robert J. Jondle
J. Preston Jones, ex officio
Roger A. Kleese
David R. MacKenzie
Terry L. Nipp
Calvin O. Qualset
James M. Tiedje

Appendix 4. Work Group Participants

Work group participants discussed the following critical issues and problems related to IPR and protection of plant materials: Work Group A—licensing, Work Group B—research and farmer exemptions, Work Group C—germplasm information and exchange, Work Group D—ethical and social issues of protection, Work Group E—research agendas, and Work Group F—synthesis and recommendations. The work groups had a chair who provided leadership and facilitated discussion and a rapporteur who was responsible for recording the group's findings. The membership of the individual work groups is listed below.

Work Group A

Neal E. De Vos, *chair*
Robert Jondle, *rapporteur*
Alan Atchley
Marco Ballarin
Clive W. Donoho
Dave Douches
Kenneth H. Evans
Doug Fisher
Robert A. Forsberg
A. Earl Foster
Barry Greengrass
Clay Logan
Laura Meagher
Bruce W. Morrissey
Eldon E. Ortman
Steve Price
Paul Sebesta
Jeffery Strachan
Donald P. Weeks

Work Group B

Mike Roth, *chair*
William H. Tallent, *rapporteur*
Fred Bliss
Robert Briggs
Richard Craig
John Gerard
Marta B. Gutierrez
Richard Hess
David Houser
Roger A. Kleese
Joseph A. Lipovsky
David Miller
James Nienhuis
Allen Norris
Thomas A. Salt
Donna Scherer
Nicholas J. Seay
Vance H. Watson
Charles F. Warren

Work Group C

Calvin D. Qualset, *chair*
Ronald Cantrell, *rapporteur*
Steve Baenziger
Joel I. Cohen
Harry B. Collins
Dawn De Vos
Steven A. Eberhart
Janet Glaser
Bryan L. Harvey
Robert E. Heiner
Dennis R. Hoerner, Jr.
David R. MacKenzie
Arturo Jose Martinez
Jerry Miksche
David Miller
Rollin G. Sears
Paul G. Sebesta
Henry L. Shands
David A. Sleper
Marsha A. Stanton
Janice M. Strachan
James C. Wesenan

Work Group D

Gary H. Heichel, *chair*
Edward Ryder, *rapporteur*
Howard J. Brooks
Larry M. Busch
Billy E. Caldwell
Beatriz Coutino
James D. Denney
Ted J. Diedrick
Tom Freetz
Burle G. Gengenbach
Jody Giesser
Neil Hamilton
Richard Hutton
J. Preston Jones
David Lambert
Ken Olson
Richard Parry
Donald N. Plucknett
Carl E. Pray
Larry Simonsmeier
Judith I. Stallmann
Deborah Strauss
Darrell Wessenberg

Work Group E

James R. Fischer, *chair*
Allan K. Stoner, *rapporteur*
John W. Dudley
Donald N. Duvick
Carl Eibl
Neal Hamilton
Charles Hess
Bruce Hunter
Edward B. Knipling
Mike Kuehn
Gary K. McCone
Robert Merrifield
Pat Moore
Charles Murphy
Lawrence Rudolph
M. Howard Silverstein
Allen Stevens
Michael S. Strauss
Charles W. Stuber
Keith A. Walker
Elizabeth C. Weimar

Work Group F

Fred Bliss, *chair*
David R. Mackenzie, *vice chair*
Jody Giesser, *vice chair*
Steve Baenziger
Robert F Barnes
Ronald Cantrell
Neal E. De Vos
Donald N. Duvick
Gary H. Heichel
Charles Hess
Robert Jondle
J. Preston Jones
Roger A. Kleese
Victor L. Lechtenberg
Richard L. Lower
Laura Meagher
Eldon E. Ortman
Edward Ryder
Henry L. Shands
M. Howard Silverstein
Allen Stevens
Charles W. Stuber
William H. Tallent

Appendix 4: List of Participants

Alan Atchley
Plant Variety Protection Office
USDA, NAL Bldg., Room 500
10301 Baltimore Blvd.
Beltsville, MD 20705

Steve Baenziger
Dept. of Agronomy
330 Keim Hall
University of Nebraska
Lincoln, NE 68583-0915

Marco Ballarin
Office of Technology Transfer
University of California
1320 Harbor Bay Pkwy. Dr. #150
Alameda, CA 94501

Robert F Barnes
Executive Vice President
ASA-CSSA-SSSA
677 South Segoe Road
Madison, WI 53711

John Barton
Professor of Law
Stanford Law School
Stanford, CA 94305

Fred Bliss
Department of Pomology
University of California
Davis, CA 95616

Robert Briggs
Crows Hybrids
P.O. Box 306
Milford, IL 60953

Howard J. Brooks
USDA/ARS/NPS
Room 133
Bldg. 005, BARC-West
Beltsville, MD 20705

Robert A. Burdett
Alabama Crop Improvement Assn.
P.O. Box 2619
Auburn, AL 36831

Larry M. Busch
Department of Sociology
Michigan State University
East Lansing, MI 48824

Billy E. Caldwell
NC Coop. Ext. Service
P.O. Box 7602
North Carolina State Univ.
Raleigh, NC 27695-7602

Ronald Cantrell
123 Agronomy Department
Iowa State University
Ames, IA 50011

Joel I. Cohen
Biotechnology & Gen. Res. Spec.
Office of Agriculture
Agency for International Development
Washington, DC 20523-1809

Harry B. Collins
Delta and Pine Land
Scott, MS 38772

Beatriz Coutino
Adv. for Biotech. Matters
Dir General de Desarrolo Tech
Azafran 18, 3er Piso
Iztacalco, Mexico

Richard Craig
Department of Horticulture
Penn State University
16 Tyson Bldg.
University Park, PA 16802

Dana G. Dalrymple
Directories for Food & Agric.
Bureau for Sci. & Tech.
U.S. Agency for Dev. Dep. of St.
Washington, DC 28502

Dawn De Vos
Harris Moran
100 Breen Road
San Juan Bautista, CA 95045

Neal E. De Vos
Elkhorn Research & Development Co., Inc.
P.O. Box 1156
Castroville, CA 95012

James O. Denney
Office of Rep. George Brown
2300 Rayburn House Office Bldg.
Washington, DC 20515

Ted J. Diedrick
Asgrow Seed Co.
The Upjohn Company
Bldg. 50
Kalamazoo, MI 49001

Machi Dilworth
DIR/BBS Room 312
National Science Foundation
1800 G Street, N.W.
Washington, DC 20550

Clive W. Donoho
Georgia Agric. Experiment Station
107 Conner Hall
University of Georgia
Athens, GA 30602

Dave Douches
Department of Crop and Soil Science
Michigan State University
East Lansing, MI 48824

John W. Dudley
S-112 Turner Hall
University of Illinois
1102 S. Goodwin Ave.
Urbana, IL 61801

Donald N. Duvick
P.O. Box 446
Johnston, IA 50131

Steven A. Eberhart
Laboratory Director
USDA-ARS-Natl. Seed Storage Lab
Colorado State University
Fort Collins, CO 80523

Carl Eibl
Mycogen
4980 Carroll Canyon Road
San Diego, CA 92121

Kenneth H. Evans
USDA Agric. Mkt. Serv., Rm. 500
NAL Bldg., 10301 Baltimore Blvd
Beltsville, MD 20705-2351

Doug Fisher
Council of Biological Editors
2100 Arch Street
Philadelphia, PA 19103

James R. Fischer
Ag Experiment Station
Clemson University
Clemson, SC 29634-0351

Robert A. Forsberg
Department of Agronomy
University of Wisconsin
Madison, WI 53706

A. Earl Foster
North Dakota State University
P.O. Box 5051
University Station
Fargo, MD 58105-5051

Gail E. Foulos
USDA-ARS-OTT
Beltsville, MD 20706

Thomas A. Fretz
Ag. & Home Econ. Experiment Station
104 Curtiss Hall
Iowa State University
Ames, IA 50011-1050

Burle G. Gengenbach
Department of Agronomy & Plant Genetics
University of Minnesota
St. Paul, MN 55108

John Gerard
J.G. Ltd., Inc.
P.O. Box M
Plymouth, IN 46563

Jody Giesser
Amoco Corporation
Suite 600
55 Shuman
Naperville, IL 60563

Janet Glaser
Biotechnology Center
University of Illinois
105 Observatory, 609 Hessel Bl.
Champaign, IL 61820

Janelle S. Graeter
USDA-ARS
Beltsville, MD 20701

Barry Greengrass
Vice Sec.-General
UPOV
34, chemin des Colombettes
CH-1211 Geneva POB, Switzerland

Marta B. Gutierrez
Unidad De Vinculacion Tecnol.
Inst. Nacional de Tech. Agro-
pecuairia, Alsina 1407 50,650
1088 Buenos Aires, Agentina

Neal Hamilton
Drake University
Agricultural Law Center
Des Moines, IA 50311

Bryan L. Harvey
Crop Science & Plant Ecology Department
University of Saskatchewan
Saskatoon, SK S7N 0W0

Gary H. Heichel
Department of Agronomy
W203 Turner
University of Illinois
1102 S. Goodwin
Urbana, IL 61801-4798

Robert E. Heiner
Nickerson American Plant Breeders, Inc.
P.O. Box 2955
Mission, KS 66201-1355

Charles Hess
College of Ag. & Env. Sci.
Department of Environmental Hort.
University of California
Davis, CA 95616

Richard J. Hess
Apartment T2
8117 Dument Drive
Vienna, VA 22180

Dennis R. Hoerner, Jr.
Associate Patent Counsel
Monsanto
700 Chesterfield Village Pkwy.
St. Louis, MO 63198

David Houser
Patent Attorney
Wisconsin Alumni Research Foundation
614 Walnut St., Rm. 1315
Madison, WI 53705

Bruce Hunter
CIBA-GEIGY Seed Division
P.O. Box 18300
Greensboro, NC 27419-8300

Richard Hutton
Conard-Pyle Company
372 Rose Hill Road
West Grove, PA 19390

Robert Jondle
Henderson & Sturm
One Pacific Place, Suite 330
1125 S. 103rd St.
Omaha, NE 68124-1076

J. Preston Jones
USDA, CSRS
Suite 330
901 D Street
Washington, DC 20250

Roger A. Kleese
Specialty Plant Products Div.
Pioneer Hi-Bred Int., Inc.
11252 Aurora Ave.
Des Moines, IA 50322

Edward B. Knipling
Deputy Administrator
USDA-ARS-NPS
Rm. 125, Bldg. 005, BARC-West
Beltsville, MD 20705

David M. Kral
ASA-CSSA-SSSA
677 South Segoe Rd.
Madison, WI 53711

Mike Kuehn
Campbell Seed
28605 County Road 104
Davis, CA 95616

David R. Lambert
American Seed Trade Assn.
601 13th Street, NW
Suite 570 S.
Washington, DC 20005

Victor L. Lechtenberg
Office of the Dean of Agriculture
Rm. 114 Ag Admin. Bldg.
Purdue University
West Lafayette, IN 47907

Joseph A. Lipovsky
USDA-ARS
Beltsville, MD 20705-2350

Clay Logan
Stark Brothers Nursery
P.O. Box 10
Louisiana, MO 63353-0010

Richard L. Lower
College of Ag. & Life Sci.
Room 136, Ag Hall
University of Wisconsin
1450 Linden Drive
Madison, WI 53706

David R. MacKenzie
USDA, CSRS
Suite 330
Aerospace Bldg.
Washington, DC 20250-2200

Arturo Jose Martinez
Inst. of Biological Resources
INTA
1712 Castelar
Prov. of BA, Argentina

Gary K. McCone
USDA
National Agricultural Library
10301 Baltimore Blvd., 5th Floor
Beltsville, MD 20705

Laura Meagher
Agric. Molecular Biol. Center
Rutgers University
P.O. Box 231
New Brunswick, NJ 08903

Robert Merrifield
Dept. Dir. of Agric. Exp. Stn.
Texas A&M University
College Station, TX 77843

Jerome P. Miksche
USDA-ARS-NPS
Plant Genome Research Program
Beltsville, MD 20705

David Miller
American Farm Bureau Red.
225 Touhy Ave.
Park Ridge, IL 68068

Pat Moore
Department of Horticulture & Landscape Architecture
Washington State University
Pullman, WA 99164

Bruce W. Morrissey
Patent Counsel, Legal Department
EI du Pont de Nemours & Co.
Barley Mill Plaza, Bldg. 36
Wilmington, DE 19880-0036

Charles Murphy
Nat'l Prog. Leader, Grain Crops
USDA/ARS, Nat'l Prog. Staff
Rm. 240, Bldg. 005, BARC-West
Beltsville, MD 20705

James Nienhuis
University of Wisconsin
Department of Horticulture
1575 Linden Dr.
Madison, WI 53706

Terry L. Nipp
123 4th Street, SE
Washington, DC 20003-1013

Allen Norris
Manager, Patents
Sandoz Crop Protection
975 California Ave.
Palo Alto, CA 94304

Ken Olson
Director of Dairy Department
American Farm Bureau
225 Touhy Ave.
Park Ridge, IL 60068

Eldon E. Ortman
Ag. Experiment Station
1140 Ag Education Bldg.
Purdue University
West Lafayette, IN 47907

Richard Parry
Deputy Assistant Administrator
USDA/ARS, OCI
Rm. 102, Bldg. 005, BARC-West
Beltsville, MD 20705

Dean Plowman
USDA-ARS
302-A Admn. Bldg.
14th & Independence Ave., SW
Washington, DC 20250

Donald N. Plucknett
The World Bank
CGIAR
1818 H Street, NW
Washington, DC 20433

Carl E. Pray
Department of Agricultural Economic
Cook College, P.O. Box 231
Rutgers University
New Brunswick, NJ 08903

Steve Price
Iowa State University
Office of Intellectual Prop. & Tech Transfer
315 Beardshear
Ames, IA 50011

Calvin O. Qualset
Department of Agronomy & Range Science
University of California
Davis, CA 95616

Ubaldo S. Rife
Embassy of Argentina
Science Attache
1600 New Hampshire Ave., NW
Washington, DC 20009

Mike Roth
Pioneer Hi-Bred Int., Inc.
700 Capital Square
400 Locust Street
Des Moines, IA 50309

J. Neil Rutger
Asst. Area Director
USDA-ARS-NSA
P.O. Box 225
Stoneville, MS 38776

Edward Ryder
U.S. Ag. Res. Station
USDA-ARS
1636 E. Alisal St.
Salinas, CA 93905

Thomas A. Salt
USDA AMS, NAL Bldg., Rm. 500
Plant Variety Protection Office
10301 Baltimore Blvd.
Beltsville, MD 20705-2351

Donna Scherer
Calgene
1920 Fifth Street
Davis, CA 95616

Rollin G. Sears
Agronomy Department
Throckmorton Hall
Kansas State University
Manhattan, KS 66506

Nicholas J. Seay
Quarles and Brady
Suite 600
1 South Pickney St.
Madison, WI 53703

Paul G. Sebesta
Texas Foundation Seed Service
Texas A&M University
College Station, TX 77843-2581

Henry L. Shands
Rm. 215, Bldg. 005
USDA-ARS
BARC-West
Beltsville, MD 20705

M. Howard Silverstein
USDA
Washington, DC 20550

Larry Simonsmeier
Washington State Patent Office
Pullman, WA 99164-1802

David A. Sleper
Department of Agronomy
210 Waters Hall
University of Missouri
Columbia, MO 65211

Judith I. Stallmann
Department of Agricultural Economics
VPI&SU
Blacksburg, VA 24060

Marsha A. Stanton
57 Walnut Avenue, Apt. A
Takoma Park, MD 20912

Allen Stevens
Petoseed Co., Inc.
37437 State Highway 16
Woodland, CA 95695

Allan K. Stoner
USDA, ARS, BA
Bldg. 001, BARC-W, Rm. 123
Beltsville, MD 20705

Janice M. Strachan
USDA AMS, NAL Bldg., Rm. 500
Plant Variety Protection Office
10301 Baltimore Blvd.
Beltsville, MD 20705-2351

Jeffery L. Strachan
USDA AMS, NAL Bldg., Rm. 500e
Plant Variety Protection Office
10301 Baltimore Blvd.
Beltsville, MD 20705-2351

Deborah G. Strauss
DIVERSITY, Genetic Resources
Communication Systems, Inc.
727 8th Street
Washington, DC 20003

Michael S. Strauss
AAAS
1333 H Street, NW
Washington, DC 20005

Charles W. Stuber
Department of Genetics
North Carolina State University
P.O. Box 7614
Raleigh, NC 27695-7614

William H. Tallent
USDA-ARS
358-A Administration Bldg.
14th & Independence Ave., SW
Washington, DC 20250

Keith A. Walker
Mycogen Corp.
4980 Carroll Canyon Rd.
San Diego, CA 92121

Charles F. Warren
U.S. Department of Commerce
Office of Patents & Trademarks
Washington, DC 20231

Roger L. Watkins
ASA-CSSA-SSSA
677 South Segoe Rd.
Madison, WI 53711

Vance H. Watson
P.O. Box 6311
Mississippi State, MS 39762

Donald P. Weeks
101 Manter Hall
University of Nebraska
Lincoln, NE 68588-0159

Elizabeth C. Weimar
Supervisory Primary Examiner
Art Unit 184, Group 180
U.S. Department of Commerce, PTO
Washington, DC 20231

Darrell Wessenberg
USDA/ARS, PWA
P.O. Box 307
Aberdeen, ID 83210

Muriel Ann Whitehead
USDA-ARS-OTT
Beltsville, MD 20705

Alvin L. Young
USDA Office of Agric. Biotech.
Washington, DC 20250-2200